TRUE TALES OF DETECTION

True Adventure Series

TRUE TALES OF DETECTION

RICHARD GARRETT

Text illustrations by Julian Graddon
Cover designed by David Bull

A Piccolo Original

PAN BOOKS LTD
LONDON

First published 1972 by Pan Books Ltd,
33 Tothill Street, London, SW1.

ISBN 0 330 23260 6

Printed in Great Britain by
Cox & Wyman Ltd,
London, Reading and Fakenham

CONTENTS

A Moment, Please . . .

This book is for your entertainment. It is about detectives and their battles against criminals. I hope you will enjoy it: personally, I have learned a good deal from writing it.

I have discovered that crime is a filthy business. Men kill, not because they are brave but usually because they are frightened. They do it in a moment of panic.

Most criminals begin their careers when they are still young. They are weak, inadequate, unintelligent, often mean people. Most of their crimes are sordid. Believe me – I know. I have studied a great many cases while gathering my material.

Once a man has been convicted, he's an outsider. Nobody wants him any more.

Look: I'm not trying to preach, but I'd like you to read this personal message from Sir John Waldron, KCVO, Commissioner of Police for the Metropolis. Sir John says:

'In these difficult times, when crime continues to be a grave social problem and the use of violence menaces our way of life, it is very important that every citizen, and in particular every young citizen, should make up his mind what his attitude to the law is going to be. The Police Service has a duty to Preserve the Queen's Peace and to maintain law and order, but it can be successful only if it has the full and active support of the general public.'

What more can one say?

R.G.

Tunbridge Wells,
1972.

ONE

MURDER IN MAYFAIR

The morning of May 6th, 1840, was chilly for late spring. At six o'clock, there was a thin mist hanging over Hyde Park. A short distance away, in Norfolk Street,* columns of blue smoke were already curling upwards from some of the chimneys. A footman opened a front door, looked briefly down the road as if searching for the postman, and then went inside again. Farther up, towards Oxford Street, a milkman's cart clattered over the cobblestones.

Number 14, which was Lord William Russell's house, was still sleeping behind closed shutters. The day, here, was in no hurry to begin. His Lordship was an old man of seventy-three, and his health was not very good. His wife had died several years earlier: now he lived with three servants. It was a quiet, rather aimless life, lacking in all sense of urgency.

At 6.30, an alarm clock jangled in one of the upper rooms of Number 14. Sarah Mancer, the housemaid, climbed reluctantly out of bed. She shivered slightly; splashed some water over her face at the wash basin; and then got dressed. Miss Mancer had been in Lord William's service for three years. She was a pleasant girl: hard-working and extremely loyal to her master.

Once she had made her bed, she padded down the

* In 1939, the name was changed to Dunraven Street to avoid confusion with another Norfolk Street in London.

Courvoisier was Lord Russell's footman

corridor to awaken the valet, a young man from Switzerland named François Courvoisier. On the way to his room she noticed a warming-pan propped up against the wall. She tut-tutted to herself. François was becoming absent-minded. It should have been placed in His Lordship's bed on the previous evening. Would the old gentleman be angry at this oversight? She doubted it. He was tired and his weariness made him tolerant. It was as if he could not be bothered to rebuke his servants.

A few nights previously, François had made the same mistake. Even though he felt the cold, Lord William had not complained. Nevertheless, Sarah made a mental note to speak to the valet about it. The young man had only been in his present job for five weeks. The afternoon before, he had forgotten to tell the coachman to pick His Lordship up at his club at five o'clock. The result was that he had been compelled to make his own way home. If this forgetfulness continued, she decided, it would not be long before the household was looking for another valet.

This, she thought, would be a pity. She liked François Courvoisier. He was a good-natured person. Even after living in London for several years he still spoke English with a strong foreign accent, and this might be why he did not say much. Or quite possibly he was shy.

She knocked on his door. 'It's a quarter to seven, François,' she said. The reply was a vague noise which might have meant 'thank you'. No doubt he was still half asleep. He was bad at getting up, and she would probably have to call him again in fifteen minutes' time. Meanwhile, she had to start the housework. She hurried downstairs to the hall.

Much to her surprise, she noticed that the front door

was open. It had been securely locked before they went to bed – she was sure of that. Now it looked as if someone had left the house in a hurry and had forgotten to close it. But who? François was in his room, Mary Hannell, the cook, would be still asleep, and it was inconceivable that Lord William had gone for a walk at this hour.

The sun had elbowed its way through the early morning clouds, and a shaft pierced the gap made by the half-opened door. Without thinking, Sarah's gaze followed it down to the carpet where it fell like a spotlight. In the centre of this splash of gold was one of His Lordship's blue evening cloaks. As if this were not unusual enough, there were a number of smaller items littered about. One of them was a silver pencil case which caught the ray and flashed it into her eyes.

She became uneasily aware that they must have been burgled. What, she wondered, ought she to do? Her life had not been very eventful, and she had never experienced a situation such as this before. Perhaps she should talk things over with Mary? Mary Hannell was older, and she would probably know how to call the police. She went upstairs and opened the door of the cook's bedroom.

'What is it?' a sleepy voice asked her. Sarah told her what she had seen. 'I don't know, I'm sure,' Mary Hannell said. 'You'd better get François. He's a man. He ought to be able to deal with it.'

For the second time in ten minutes, Sarah presented herself at the valet's room. To her surprise, he opened the door at once. Normally he would still have been in his dressing gown, but today he was fully dressed. He had shaved, his shoes were brightly polished, and his hair was neatly smoothed down.

Together they went down to the hall. Courvoisier closed the front door. Then he knelt down to examine the objects on the floor. In addition to the pencil case, there was a small jewel box, a pair of opera glasses, a toothpick with a gold tip, a silver spoon, one of Mary Hannell's thimbles, and a pair of spectacles. There was also a towel, and it looked as if the thief had made up a kind of parcel. In his hurry to get away, he had dropped it, and the contents had spilled out onto the carpet.

Courvoisier shook his head. Without saying anything, he went upstairs. Sarah followed him.

There were two sitting-rooms on this floor. The one at the front of the house was seldom used. In the old days, Lady Russell had done most of her entertaining here, but there was very little social life nowadays. When he was at home, His Lordship spent most of his time in the smaller room at the back. It was more like a study, with large bookcases, a comfortable armchair, and a small desk by the window.

Whilst the burglar did not seem to have taken anything from the front room, he had obviously been busy in the study. The desk had been moved, and one of the drawers wrenched open. A large screwdriver, which presumably had acted as a jemmy, lay on the chair. There was a bunch of keys on the floor.

Courvoisier seemed to be very upset by the crime. He turned to Sarah and, with a sigh, said: 'Oh, God! Somebody must have robbed us.'

It was not the practical, man-of-the-world reaction she had hoped for. She refrained from telling him that this was pretty obvious and, instead, suggested: 'Let's go and see where My Lord is.'

There was little doubt about where His Lordship

was. He was never called before eight o'clock and, since the time was only a few minutes before seven, he was, presumably, still asleep.

As they walked to his bedroom Sarah thought again how shaken the valet seemed to be by the turn of events. Normally, he carried himself erectly and had a rather quick step. Now, his shoulders were hunched and his always pale face seemed to be whiter than ever. Without knocking, he pushed open the door. He went over to the windows and opened the shutters, while Sarah tip-toed towards the four-poster bed. As the daylight poured in, she caught sight of her master and instantly let out a scream.

Lord William Russell's face was covered by a towel but there was no mistaking what had happened. The towel and the pillow were both drenched with blood. Whoever had broken in during the night had not been content with theft. Lord William Russell had been murdered.

The three servants, joined a few minutes later by the coachman who lived in the mews at the back, knocked on neighbours' doors in a state of near panic. Amid the confusion, somebody ran round to the nearest police station, and reported the crime. Inspector John Tedman was on duty at the time. Giving some instructions to the sergeant, he walked quickly round to Number 14. Courvoisier was waiting in the hall. In his accented English, he told the Inspector what had happened.

'I think you should see the back door,' he suggested.

They walked down a flight of stairs, past the kitchen and the pantry which was Courvoisier's headquarters, and along the short passage leading to the rear of the building. The door was open, and Tedman noticed that there were some marks on it. Apparently, it had been forced. The intruder's task must have been made easier by the fact that the bolt had become rusted into position. It had obviously been a long time since anyone had used it.

'What's out there?' Tedman asked.

'A yard, some stables and a wall.'

'We'd better have a look at them.'

His first thought was that the thief had climbed over the stable roof. But if he had done this, some of the slates would have been dislodged or even broken. So far as he could see, they were all in good order.

The wall was fairly high but it might have been possible to scale it. Tedman asked Courvoisier to bring him a ladder. He climbed to the top and saw, as he had expected, a thick layer of dust. Since it had not rained for several days, it had lain there undisturbed. If somebody had clambered over it, there would surely be some marks. There were none – and nor were there any on the gate which, unlike the back door, had not been tampered with.

How, then, had the thief got in?

'We'll go to the bedroom now,' Tedman told the valet.

The police surgeon had just completed his examination. He explained that Lord William's throat had been cut with a sharp knife, and that he had been asleep at the time. The killer had covered his face with a hand towel, presumably in an effort to stem the flow of blood. There was no sign of any weapon.

Tedman made a careful examination of the room. A book lay open on the floor beside the bed. A pair of spectacles were resting on it. On the bedside table, a nightlight had burnt one-third of the way down. About six feet away, on a bookshelf between the two windows, a candle had burnt out completely.

While the detective was looking around, Courvoisier had sat down in one of the chairs. He was now muttering to himself unhappily: 'Oh, dear – this is a shocking job. I shall lose my place and my character.'

'Never mind that,' Tedman said. 'I want you to see if anything seems to be missing.'

The valet glanced vaguely at the bedside table. There was an empty watch stand on it. 'There's one thing,' he said. 'His Lordship's gold watch has gone.'

Tedman picked up an empty wallet from the dressing table. 'Do you know if there was any money in this?'

'Yesterday he put a £10 and a £5 note in it. Is it empty?'

'It's empty.'

Tedman then pointed to the book and spectacles on the floor. 'What are those doing there?'

'I left his Lordship reading in bed when I went off duty,' the valet said.

'That book?'

'I think so – yes.'

At the foot of the bed, a dressing case had been forced open. Courvoisier said that it had contained four tobacco pipes, a pair of opera glasses and five gold rings. The pipes were still there. The opera glasses were presumably those which had been found lying on the hall carpet. The rings were missing.

On another table, there was a Russian leather box. It contained a gold ring, a spectacle case, two copper coins and four small cylindrical cases which were used for carrying gold sovereigns. They were all empty.

'Right,' the detective said. 'We'll have a look at the study now.'

Meanwhile Inspector Peirse of 'A' Division had been questioning Sarah Mancer and Mary Hannell.

'I want,' he told the two women, 'to find out everything that happened here yesterday. What did His Lordship do, for instance?'

Sarah Mancer said that he had eaten his breakfast at nine o'clock at usual. He spent the morning pottering about the house and, at one o'clock, had gone off to his club. He had told Courvoisier to send his carriage round for him at five o'clock and the valet had forgotten. His Lordship had returned home at five-thirty in a hired hackney cab. No, he did not seem to be angry at what had happened.

And in the evening? His Lordship had been in his study, reading. He went to bed at about 11.30.

Had there been any visitors? Two men had called to mend a bell, and Courvoisier had received a friend for tea at about five o'clock. His name, Mary Hannell thought, was Carr. He had worked with the valet in his previous job. No – they did not hear the conversation, but it hadn't lasted for long. Carr was gone by six.

And nobody else?

Nobody else.

What had been their own movements? All three of them had taken dinner at one o'clock. Mary Hannell had gone out in the evening, and Sarah Mancer and Courvoisier had eaten supper on their own. When Miss Hannell returned at ten, Courvoisier had opened the front door for her. After that, he had locked, chained and bolted it. They knew this for a fact since he had the key in his hand. Miss Hannell then sat down to supper and made some remark about how nice it would be to have a glass of beer. Very sportingly, they considered, Courvoisier had gone round to a nearby public house where he bought her a bottle. After supper, they had all gone to bed.

A police sergeant who had been searching the servants' quarters reported that he had found nothing of any importance. But when an inventory was taken of the silver plate in the valet's pantry, a number of silver spoons and forks were found to be missing.

The nation was scandalized by the murder of Lord William Russell. Contemporary newspapers described the killer as 'brutal', 'cowardly' and 'an inhuman monster'. Much was made of the fact that the victim was a frail old man who, even if he had been awake, would have been unable to defend himself. Furthermore, in the opinion of several editors, the crime was made even more appalling by the fact that he was a member of the aristocracy. In the very class-conscious Victorian age, it was more villainous to shed blue blood than the more commonplace, red, variety!

The man ultimately responsible for the investigation was Richard Mayne, one of two commissioners in charge of the Metropolitan Police Force. Mayne was tough, extremely efficient, and a martinet. Under his leadership, the Force, which Sir Robert Peel had founded in 1829, had become a well organized and highly disciplined body of men. His office was in a street running off Whitehall called Great Scotland Yard. It was here that, a year or so after Lord William's murder, the CID was established.

Inspector Peirse had the duty of telling Commissioner Mayne about the crime. The latter made it clear that he wanted results quickly. With the Government and the House of Lords taking an interest in the case, and with the Press stirring up public opinion, a long-drawn-out investigation would be intolerable.

After he had listened to Peirse's account of things, the Commissioner explained that he was inclined to rule out the idea of an intruder. He repeated Tedman's observations that there were no marks on the wall at the back of the premises. And why had Lord William been killed in his bed – and, furthermore, asleep? This certainly did not suggest that he had disturbed the burglar. Indeed, the murder was the strangest aspect of the entire case. Why *had* anyone wished to kill Lord William?

'But, sir,' Peirse said, '*somebody* must have disturbed the man. How, otherwise, can we account for the situation in the hall? It looks as if he dropped some of the swag in a panic and bolted out of the front door.'

'Perhaps that is what you are supposed to think,' Mayne suggested. 'Isn't it possible that the back door was forced from the inside, and that the goods were scattered about in the hall, to make you think that somebody broke into the house? Wouldn't that be quite a good way of putting us off the scent?'

Peirse agreed that it might be. 'What do you suggest we do next, sir?' he asked.

Mayne advised him and Tedman to find out some more about Lord William's habits. Why, for instance, had the nightlight only burnt one-third of the way down when one would have expected it to have been alight all night? And what was that candle doing on the bookcase? The valet had said that it was for His Lordship to read by in bed. But – six feet away? It might just as well have been in the hall.

'There's a man named Ellis,' Mayne said. 'He used to

be Lord William's valet before Courvoisier was employed. I believe he is now in the Earl of Mansfield's service. You might also talk to the man named Carr. If he worked with Courvoisier in his previous job, he may be able to tell you about him.'

Two policemen remained at 14 Norfolk Street. One was instructed to keep an eye on the three servants who were all confined to the house for the time being. The other was told to search the premises thoroughly in case any of the stolen objects came to light. Tedman went off to interview Ellis whilst Peirse made it his duty to see Carr.

Ellis turned out to be an amiable man who was shocked by the death of his late master. He was only too anxious to help.

'What can I do?' he asked.

'Tell me about Lord Russell. Did he always have a nightlight burning on his bedside table?'

'Latterly – yes. Sometimes His Lordship got up in the night. If there was no light, he was apt to fall over the furniture.'

'And so he would keep it burning all night? By the morning, the nightlight would have been used up?'

'Just so.'

'And so,' Tedman continued, 'If the nightlight had only burnt one-third of the way down, somebody else must have extinguished it?'

'Most definitely,' Ellis said. 'His Lordship would never blow it out.'

And that, Inspector Tedman told himself, fixes the time of the crime. Whoever blew out the nightlight must have been the murderer. We merely have to establish when Lord Russell went to sleep, and how long it takes one-third of a nightlight to burn its way down. After that, it's an easy piece of arithmetic. To Ellis he said;

'Would you mind telling me about candles? One was found on a bookshelf about six feet from the bed. His Lordship had used it to read a book in bed, and he forgot to snuff it out. When we searched the room this morning, we found that it had completely burnt out.'

Ellis was looking puzzled, 'Inspector,' he said, 'are you sure that your observations were correct? About the book and the candle, I mean.'

Tedman said that he had seen them with his own eyes.

'Then I cannot understand it,' Ellis said. 'For one thing, Lord Russell never, under any circumstances, read in bed. And, for another, His Lordship had an unusual fear of fire. My last duty, on seeing him comfortably settled for the night, was always to blow out the candle and remove it. The idea of his leaving a candle burning in the room is completely impossible. I'm sorry, but I have to say this.'

'Thank you,' Tedman said. 'Is there anything else you can tell me?'

'Only what I heard,' Ellis said. 'There was the matter of His Lordship's locket.'

Ellis recalled a gold locket which Lord Russell always carried in one of his pockets. It contained a lock of Lady Russell's hair, and he was tremendously attached to it.

Recently, however, he had been down to Richmond on a short visit to some relatives. Courvoisier and a groom had accompanied him, and they had stayed at a hotel called the Castle Tavern. When he returned home, Lord Russell found that the locket was missing. He assumed that it had fallen out of his pocket, and he wrote to the hotel manager – asking him to look for it. In due course a letter arrived saying that they had searched everywhere, and had found no sign of it.

'You are suggesting,' Tedman said, 'that it must have been stolen?'

'It seems like it, doesn't it?' Ellis said. 'Of course, one of the hotel staff may have taken a fancy to it.'

'You are implying that it could have been Courvoisier?' Tedman suggested.

'It is not for me to say,' Ellis said.

Carr doubted very much whether he could assist the inquiry. He told Inspector Peirse that he had not known Courvoisier well. 'He was a quiet bloke, if you understand me,' he said. 'I liked him, of course – all of us did. But I can't say we really knew him.'

'What made him change his job?' Peirse asked.

Carr smiled. 'Why do any of us change?' he said. 'To get more money, I suppose.'

'You mean Lord Russell offered him better wages?'

'Now that I cannot say,' Carr replied. 'You'd have thought so, wouldn't you? But there were two remarks he let slip, which make me doubt it.'

'And what were they?'

'He once told me that he was very unlucky to have changed from his last place to the present. The way he put it was that he'd been given a sovereign and got seventeen shillings for it. You can make of that what you like.'

'You mean that the wages were higher, but he had to work harder for them?'

'Perhaps. He told me: "I know that old Billy (he was referring to His Lordship, if you understand me); if I had a half or one-third of his property, I should no longer be in this country" '

'In other words, he disliked Lord Russell?'

'I wouldn't say that,' Carr replied. 'I doubt if he ever disliked anybody.'

'Do you think Courvoisier is capable of killing a man?'

'I am sure he isn't,' Carr said. 'He's the most mild, inoffensive person.'

May 6th had been a Wednesday. On the Friday, there were two sensational discoveries at 14 Norfolk Street. The police, ferreting away diligently, found a gold ring and a gold seal hidden near the sink in Courvoisier's pantry. On that day, too, details of a reward were published in a newspaper called the *Gazette*. For any information which might help the police to find the murderer, the Government were offering £200 and Lord Russell's family were prepared to pay another £200.

On the following day, the gold locket with the curl of Lady Russell's hair in it was found near the fire-place in the pantry. It must have been there for several days, for it was covered with a film of dust.

By the 10th, when a medal issued to soldiers who had fought at Waterloo was found in the pantry and then, later on, a number of sovereigns turned up, Inspector Peirse decided that the time had come to take Courvoisier into custody.

Throughout the investigation, Commissioner Mayne had been in close touch with his detectives. It was small wonder, for even the Royal family was said to be concerned about a crime which had resulted in the death of such a distinguished nobleman. Nowadays, it would not have been a difficult case to solve, in 1840, however, the police had little to work with. The art of fingerprints, for example, had yet to be developed, and the tools of a detective's trade were his magnifying glass and his common sense. It was one thing to know who had committed a particular crime. It was often much more difficult to prove it.

Proof, indeed, was the subject of a conversation between Mayne and Peirse in the former's office during the second week in June.

'You're sure this man Courvoisier did it?' Mayne asked.

'Beyond any reasonable doubt,' the Inspector said. 'We discovered nearly all the loot hidden in his pantry, and there was that matter of the gloves.'

'The gloves?' Mayne asked.

'I told you about it at the time, sir,' Peirse said. 'It was after Courvoisier had been taken to Newgate. His uncle came round to the house and asked if he could take his nephew some clean linen. Tedman said that he was going round to the prison on the following morning and that he would take it with him. The man wanted a shirt, a pair of socks, and some underwear.

'Tedman was making up a parcel, and he took a shirt out of the wardrobe. As he did so, a pair of gloves fell out. They were stained with blood.'

'Ah yes – I remember,' the Commissioner said. 'But somebody else could have put them there. After all, no gloves were discovered when you searched his room shortly after the crime.'

'Possibly, sir – but then there was the carving knife. You will recall – we found a set of four, each of them with an ivory handle. The blade of one was duller than the others and it had a patch of what looked like rust on it. We are almost sure that this was blood. I am convinced that it was the murder weapon.'

'It may have been, but that does not mean to say that Courvoisier was the man who used it. I tell you, Peirse, I'm worried about this. Nearly all the evidence is circumstantial, and the betting is that Courvoisier will be acquitted when his case comes up for trial next week. Indeed, I understand that one gentleman has offered him a job when he's released, and some others are getting up a fund to pay for his defence. What's more, this is going to be the most highly publicized trial of this century. They tell me that several members of the aristocracy are going to attend. We shall look very stupid if our man gets off – shan't we, Peirse?'

'Yes, sir,' said the Inspector.

'Tell me one thing more. Are you certain that *all* the stolen property has been recovered?'

'No, sir – not all of it. There are still some silver spoons and forks to be accounted for. They are certainly nowhere in 14 Norfolk Street: we've searched every corner of the house. They might be anywhere, I'm afraid.'

'Then let us hope,' the Commissioner said, 'that the counsel for the prosecution does a good job. I cannot say that I envy him.'

The courtroom at the Old Bailey was packed to capacity. The Duke of Sussex was there, and so were Their Graces the Earls of Sheffield, Scarborough, River, Cadogan, Lucan and Charleville. There were barons and baronesses almost, it seemed, by the score; the ambassadors of Holland, Portugal and Bavaria; and as many members of the common public that could secure admission. It may not have been the most sensational trial of the century: it was certainly the most fashionable.

Courvoisier cut a neat figure in the dock. His manner suggested the harmless, inoffensive qualities that had impressed his friends, and he was immaculately turned out in well-laundered white linen and a smart cutaway jacket. Through the first day's proceedings he gave no sign of any emotion and the general opinion was that he seemed to be optimistic.

In spite of a long and spirited speech by the prosecution, the police were by no means confident of the outcome and, by the end of the day, the odds seemed still to be in favour of an acquittal. But then, that evening, the whole situation changed dramatically.

Commissioner Richard Mayne had just finished dinner, when a messenger called at his house. Would he go at once to Marlborough Street police station? It was, the man stressed, most urgent and it had to do with the Courvoisier case.

Mayne needed no further bidding. When he reached the station, he found two people waiting for him. One was a French woman who kept an hotel in Leicester Square. The other was a solicitor from a firm in the City. There was also a parcel done up in brown paper.

'This lady is Madame Piclaine,' the solicitor said. 'She does not read the English newspapers and that is why she had not come forward before. Apparently a newspaper in Paris carried an article about the case. This was seen by one of her partners, who told her about it. She knows Courvoisier – he used to work for her.'

'In what way?' Mayne asked.

The woman spoke volubly in a mixture of French and

English. Courvoisier had come to her hotel, she explained, five years ago. He wanted a job as a waiter and, since they had a vacancy, they took him on. For some reason, they never called him by his real name, but always referred to him as 'John'.

Presently, he moved on to another job and that, they imagined, was likely to be the last they saw of him. But then, two days before the murder, he turned up unexpectedly at the hotel. He had with him a parcel, and he asked whether he might leave it there until the following Tuesday. Mme Piclaine agreed; the parcel was put in a cupboard and she thought no more about it.

When she heard the account in the French newspaper, and read about the reward, she remembered the parcel. It occurred to her that it had never been collected, and she took it down from the shelf. On her partner's advice, she went by hackney cab to the City and handed it over to her solicitor. When the latter opened it, he found that there were several silver spoons and forks inside and that each of them bore Lord William's family crest.

Mayne thanked her and said that she had done well. 'But now,' he said, 'I shall have to ask you to come with me to Newgate prison. We have to be sure that this man you call "John" and Courvoisier are the same person.'

Seldom have the forces of law and order worked faster. An identification parade was held at the prison, and Mme Piclaine immediately pointed to Courvoisier. 'That's him,' she said. 'That's John.'

Meanwhile another investigation was taking place. One of the detectives, on the advice of Sarah Minter, went to the home of a shopkeeper who sold prints. He had with him the brown paper in which the parcel of silver cutlery had been wrapped. 'I have reason to believe that this came from your shop,' the inspector said.

The retailer looked at it carefully. 'Yes – that is correct. We have a special design on our paper. There's no mistaking it.'

'Have you ever sold a print to Lord William Russell?'

'I have sold him many. The last time was shortly before he was killed. It had a religious theme. "The Vision of Ezekiel", the artist had entitled it. A charming picture.'

'You would swear to this in a court of law?'

'Most certainly,' the dealer said.

'Then please do so tomorrow,' the detective asked.

The discovery of the missing spoons and forks and Mme Piclaine's identification changed the situation completely. After a trial lasting three days, François Courvoisier was found guilty of the murder of Lord William Russell, and was sentenced to death. Ten days later, he was publicly hanged at Newgate in front of an audience which was only marginally less distinguished than that which had attended his trial.

To all intents and purposes, the case had ended on the first night of the trial. Once he heard about the discovery of the missing cutlery and had been identified by Mme Piclaine, Courvoisier asked to see his solicitor. The two men met in his cell, and the valet made his confession.

It seemed that he had been stealing from Lord Russell for some time. On the night of the murder, His Lordship had felt ill and had come downstairs. Hearing noises in the pantry, he came to see what was happening. He discovered Courvoisier in the act of concealing some gold rings behind the skirting.

His Lordship gave way to a rare moment of anger. He charged his valet with robbing him and said that he would dismiss him the following morning. Then he returned to bed and fell asleep. Courvoisier crept into his room and cut the old man's throat. He blew out the nightlight, but left his own candle behind. In attempting to make it seem as if somebody had broken in, he completely forgot about the wall at the back of the house, and made the additional mistake of forcing the door from the inside. Why did he indulge in such unnecessary details as making it appear that Lord William had been reading in bed? He could give no explanation.

Perhaps the truth of the matter was best summed up in one newspaper, which observed that 'Courvoisier was hanged by his own foolishness'.

TWO

ROBBERY AT THE ROADSIDE

If the methods of detection used in the investigation of
Lord William Russell's murder seem unscientific by
today's standards, those used by Eugène-François
Vidocq, three decades earlier, appear primitive. Nevertheless, as numerous criminals found to their cost, they
were effective. Vidocq nearly always got his man
through perseverance and a good deal of cunning.

He was a thickset individual of medium height with
enormous shoulders. His face, which was open and
friendly, was often obscured by disguises. Sometimes,
indeed, it seemed that he had a passion for dressing up.
He once caught a murderer by pretending to be a
very old man. On another occasion, he put on a nun's
habit and passed himself off as a mother superior. Im-
probably, for he was very masculine-looking, he got
away with it.

This master detective had not always been on the side
of the law. He was quick tempered, reckless and an
expert swordsman. At the age of fifteen, he killed a
fencing master in a duel. For the next fifteen years, although he never robbed anybody, he was continually in
and out of prison. The authorities put him in: Vidocq
got himself out (escaping was another of his talents).

Whenever he regained his liberty, he found, as so
many other ex-convicts have done, that it was very
difficult to lead an honest life. The police were con-

tinually trying to re-arrest him. And the criminal world regarding him as part of itself, attempted to get him to join in its schemes.

In an attempt to come to terms with law and order Vidocq finally volunteered to become a police spy. He was so successful that, in 1817, he was invited to form an organization known as the Sûreté. Very roughly, it is the equivalent of the CID in England. During the course of his career as a detective, he was given credit for something like 750 arrests. His assistants, like himself, were mostly men who had graduated from the prison floor.

One method that Vidocq sometimes used was to disguise himself as a criminal. He adopted the name 'Jules' and often joined the very gang that he intended to break up. On at least one occasion, he even helped to plan the crime. Then he alerted the police agents. When the robbers moved in, they found that 'Jules' had vanished, and that a posse of policemen was waiting for them.

One of Vidocq's more sensational cases concerned a series of robberies on the approach roads to Paris. One of the victims, a poultry dealer, had been killed. Normally, the police have a fairly good idea of who is responsible for a particular crime. Each crook has his own style: the problem, in most cases, is to find the proof.

In this instance, however, none of the suspected persons seemed to be guilty. The police kept a watch on all their movements, but none of them did anything illegal. And, in the meanwhile, the robberies continued. Things were rapidly getting to a state when people were scared of travelling to Paris by night.

In view of the situation, the actions of a butcher named Fontaine were, perhaps, surprising. M. Fontaine had decided to travel the forty miles from Paris to a town named Corbeil, where a fair was being held. Among the attractions was a sale of cattle, and he was hoping to make some purchases. Consequently, he took with him a leather bag containing 1,500 francs.

All this is reasonable enough, but what possessed Fontaine to set off in the evening? He must have known about the highway robberies. Surely, he was asking for trouble?

It was a cold winter's night, and he had not gone very far, when he stopped at an inn for a glass of wine. There were two fairly well-dressed customers already in the bar and he fell into conversation with them.

'Where are you going?' one of them asked.

The butcher told them.

'That's a pretty fair way. Aren't you worried about these robberies that have been taking place?'

Fontaine admitted that he was.

'It's a funny coincidence,' the other customer said. 'We're going to Corbeil, too. Why don't we all go together? It might be safer that way.'

The three of them set off down the road and, after an hour, they came to another inn. Fontaine invited his new friends to join him for dinner. They ate well and had some more wine. He was beginning to enjoy himself. These were excellent companions: their talk was amusing and, he considered, they would be more than a match for any highwaymen.

By the time they had finished their meal, the night was pitch black without so much as a wafer of moon. Fontaine walked on ahead with one of the men, whilst the other brought up the rear.

They were talking about life in Paris when suddenly something crashed down on the butcher's head. A vivid

streak of light flashed across the backs of his eyes. His
skull seemed to be falling in. For a second, he blacked
out. Then, clinging desperately to consciousness, he
swung round. The man at the back had his stick raised
for another blow, but Fontaine lashed out. More by luck
than anything else, his boot homed on one of the villain's shins. It knocked him off balance and his stick
swished harmlessly through the air. He recovered himself, and struck out again. This time, he caught Fontaine's shoulder with such force that it knocked him to
the ground.

While all this had been taking place, the second man
had drawn a dagger. Once the luckless Fontaine was
down, he fell upon him. He stabbed him in the shoulder,
but the butcher was not yet beaten. He fought back with
a rabbit punch to the side of the neck. His assailant
seemed to pause for a second, shake his head, and then
delivered the second thrust with the knife. This time, it
caught Fontaine in the arm. All told, the butcher was
wounded four times before, at last, he fell into uncon-
sciousness.

The two men picked up the leather bag with the 1,500
francs in it, glanced down at their victim, assumed that
he was dead and then walked back towards Paris. One
of them was limping rather badly from the kick on his
shin.

But Fontaine was far from dead. He must have been
unusually tough, for the first blow would have been
enough to fracture an average skull. Before very long,
the cold night air brought him back to his senses. His
knife wounds were hurting, and his head ached ap-
pallingly. He began to groan.

The sound of his distress attracted a farmer who was
walking back to his house. He went to investigate: saw

the stricken butcher, and hurried to the nearest village
for help. Within a short space of time, Fontaine had
been taken to hospital. Two days later, the surgeon said
that he was out of danger.

When the case was reported to Vidocq, he rubbed his
hands with delight. Here, at last, was a victim who had
survived an attack by the robbers. Now, after four
months of frustration, he might hope for some real evidence.

They were standing on top of a small hill on the road
from Paris to Corbeil. A brisk wind was shaking the
upper branches of a nearby clump of trees. Ahead of
them, the countryside stretched out in a beautiful pattern
of woods, ploughed fields and meadows.

A party of men was searching the ground. One of
them was collecting buttons that had been ripped off a
jacket. Another was making careful drawings of foot-
prints. The third was collecting pieces of paper which,
for some unaccountable reason, were littered about the
place.

On the edge of the group, Eugène-François Vidocq
stood with his shoulders hunched, gazing down at the
ground. Did he believe that, if he stared at it for long
enough, he could find some vital clue to the case? Why
not? He was brilliant at extracting confessions. Perhaps
he could persuade the very grass to talk.

He kicked a fallen twig, muttered something to himself, and turned to one of the agents.

'How many do you think were here?' he asked.

'An army, by the look of it,' the man said. 'No – I
don't think that's true. There's been a scuffle. Three or
four, probably.'

Vidocq grunted and resumed his study of the grass. A

few minutes later the agent who had been examining the bits of paper came over to him. 'There's something interesting here,' he said. Most of the fragments were coated with blood, and it looked as if this particular piece had been used to wipe the blade of a knife.

'Do you see – some writing?'

It was hard to decipher. Part of it had been torn off, and the rest was spattered with spots of blood. It seemed to be an address – but whose? If it belonged to the butcher, they would not be very much farther forward.

'I'm going back to headquarters,' Vidocq said. 'Keep on searching.'

Back in his office and with the help of a magnifying glass, he managed to string the words together. It looked like:

A Monsieur Rao (then came the jagged edge, where the rest of the word had been ripped away)
Wine Merchant, bar
Roche
Cli

'And what,' Vidocq asked, 'is one supposed to make of that?'

He took a map of Paris down from the wall, and studied it carefully. He began with the enigmatic 'Cli'. What place names began with those three letters? Clignancourt? Chauseé de Clignancourt – Clignancourt Road? It was a possibility. He called to a clerk. 'Can you think of anything beginning with "Roche" on the Clignancourt Road?'

The man thought for a minute or two. Then: 'The

Barrière Rochechouart,' he said. 'That's somewhere near there.'

'Thank you,' Vidocq said. He took a sheet of paper and wrote: 'Chauseé de Clignancourt, Barrière Roche-chouart, Wine Merchant, À Monsieur Rao . . .' A wine merchant whose name began with Rao. It shouldn't be difficult.

There was also the testimony of Fontaine, who had recovered and was telling people how he had caught one of the villains a severe blow on the shin. If the wine merchant limped, it would be so much the better. Or, perhaps, the criminal was a customer of this M. Rao . . . That would make it more difficult, but at least they had *something* to go on.

'Come on,' he said to two of his colleagues. 'We're going to have a drink in the Chaussée de Clig-nancourt.'

A policeman must be patient, and Vidocq was nothing if not that. They found the wine shop without difficulty and noticed that the proprietor's name was Raoul. He was out of Paris, staying at a small house he owned in the country. A waiter said that he would be away for two or three days.

There was only one thing to do – wait. Agents were posted at suitable points. Vidocq himself went to a couple of shops in the vicinity, where he asked some questions about Raoul. After that, he waited in a door-way for the rest of the day. Towards evening, the wine shop became fairly busy, but none of the customers limped. Nor were any of them known to the police. Indeed, they looked a reasonably law abiding collection of men.

It was not until four o'clock on the following after-noon, that one of the watchers came over to Vidocq.

'Did you see who's just gone in?' he asked. 'Surely, it was Court? Did you notice how he limped?'

Court was a man who had been arrested by Vidocq some while previously. He had been sentenced to six months for armed robbery. The detective remembered thinking that he had got off very lightly.

'See where he lives,' Vidocq told one of his agents. Then he went back to his office.

Later that afternoon, he was in conference with the attorney-general.

'This wine merchant – Raoul,' the latter asked. 'Is there any reason to suspect him?'

'I've been making a few inquiries,' Vidocq said. 'His brother-in-law was convicted of smuggling some time ago.'

'That doesn't make him a criminal. And you say that most of his customers seemed to be fairly decent people.'

'Nevertheless, his place does have a bad reputation in the neighbourhood. Court is certainly one of his regulars.'

'We've no evidence on Court.'

'With his record and the fact that he limps? We don't need very much.'

Outside the attorney-general's office, the agent who had followed Court was waiting for Vidocq.

'Well?'

'It's a house in the Rue Coquenard. He and his wife live on the first floor.'

'Detail four of the boys. We'll pay him a visit at dawn tomorrow morning.'

When Vidocq arrived at the house, there was a smudge of light in the sky. It was a cold morning with patches of ice on the pavement. The building badly

Vidocq had a call to make in the Rue Coquenard

needed painting, and there was a smell of cabbage on the stairs.

'Be as quiet as you can,' he said to the other detectives.

When they reached the first-floor landing, Vidocq gestured to the others to wait at the top of the stairs, while he went over and knocked at the door.

Presently, he heard a shuffle of feet. Then a voice, which was still slurred slightly by sleep, asked: 'Who's there?'

If his colleagues had been able to make out Vidocq's face in the gloom of the landing, they would have seen that he was smiling. In a voice which was not a bit like his own, he said: 'Who should it be? Raoul, of course. Come on and open the door.'

They heard the rattle of a lock, and the door was cautiously opened. 'Well!' the man who was Court exclaimed. 'What's new? Has anything fresh turned up?'

Still using his strange voice, Vidocq said: 'Yes, yes. I have a thousand things to say to you.' He then beckoned to the others, and the five of them went into the room.

In contrast to the half-light of the landing, it was quite bright inside. When Court discovered who his visitor was, he looked alarmed. His wife, who was quickly putting a coat on over her nightdress, seemed even more troubled.

'Well, well – if it isn't M. Jules,' Court said – using Vidocq's underworld name. 'What can I do for you?' He limped back into the room to offer the detective a chair.

'I see you've hurt your leg,' Vidocq said. 'You want to be more careful.'

'Yes,' Court said. 'I sprained it.'

'Search the room, boys,' Vidocq said to his men.

It did not take them long to find several pistols and a number of knives. Vidocq smiled. 'You'll have plenty of time to rest your leg,' he said. And, to two of his detectives: 'Take them both to the nearest police station.'

It was a Sunday morning, and church bells were summoning Parisians to mass, when Vidocq went round to the wine shop. The shutters were up and the front door was bolted. Vidocq knocked on it. Presently, it was opened by a waiter.

'Is Raoul in?' Vidocq asked.

'He has spent the night at his country place,' the waiter said. 'We expect him back about nine.'

'Then I'll wait,' Vidocq said. 'Perhaps you'll bring me a cup of coffee.'

It was after twelve, in fact, before the proprietor returned. A waiter ran out to meet him. Vidocq could hear him say: 'Who wants me?' And then, as he came into the shop, he seemed to recognize Vidocq. Just as Court had done, he greeted him with his underworld name of M. Jules.

'What brings you here?' he asked.

Vidocq was at his cunning best. 'There have been accusations,' he said. And then, impulsively: 'But this is no place for a conversation. The police want to talk to you, you see. Nothing serious. It's about some of your customers, as a matter of fact. The neighbours have been saying that political meetings are held here. People wanting to overthrow the Government. Sheer nonsense, probably.'

Raoul smiled. He had clearly believed every word that Vidocq had spoken. 'Is that all?' he said. 'Let's go to headquarters at once. You looked so suspicious at first, that anyone might have thought I'd committed a murder.'

Vidocq admitted afterwards that the man seemed to be so confident and had made the remark about murder so casually that he began to have doubts about his guilt.

'Just one thing before we go,' he said. 'You won't mind if we search the premises?'

'Is that necessary?' Raoul asked.

'A formality. They say that some seditious literature may be hidden here. Jokes against the Government. Rubbish, no doubt.'

In an upstairs room there was a small desk. It was locked. Vidocq asked for the keys, and Raoul handed them to him. 'You won't find anything in there,' he said.

'Probably not,' Vidocq agreed.

The wine-shop proprietor watched with apparent indifference as Vidocq thumbed his way through a pile of bills and letters. None of them seemed to be of any importance and he was about to give up. Then a fragment of paper caught his attention. He slowly pulled it out from the desk and began to study it carefully. It was a sheet of paper from which a corner had been ripped off. What was left of the address perfectly matched the fragment which had been found on the road to Corbeil.

Raoul's look of indifference had now vanished. As Vidocq later wrote: 'A ghastly paleness came over him; and springing towards a drawer in which were his loaded pistols, he endeavoured to seize them.'

But the wily detective had been expecting the sudden movement. He grabbed Raoul before he could get hold of the guns and fastened his wrists.

'As I said at the beginning,' he observed, 'this is no place for conversation. We'd better go to the police station.'

It was a few minutes before midnight. The room was unheated and badly lit by a candle. A rough wooden chair provided the only furnishing and, on this, Raoul sat huddled. He had been there for over ten hours without any food, and he was very hungry.

Vidocq was only a few yards away in a pleasantly warm office, carefully working out the next phase of his attack. Raoul had been locked in one cell. Court and his wife were sitting in similarly unhappy circumstances in another. They had hardly spoken a word to each other since the door had been slammed shut. Mrs Court was shivering from the cold. Her husband was gazing straight ahead, apparently deep in thought. It was as if his wife no longer existed.

If Court and Raoul were worried, so, to a lesser extent, was Vidocq. He was now reasonably certain who had been responsible for the robberies, but he had to admit that the evidence was largely circumstantial. Raoul's action, and the incriminating piece of the letter, might be enough to secure a conviction – but what did he have on Court?

That he had spent a term in prison for armed robbery? That he limped? Plenty of people did that. That he frequented Raoul's wine shop? But, then, so did all his other customers. What else was there? Firearms and knives on the premises? Possibly – but there was nothing to show that they had been used. Vidocq decided that his only hope was to get a confession out of him. He told a policeman to bring the suspects in.

Vidocq had many talents and by no means the least

of them was as an actor. If he had decided to go on the stage, he would doubtless have done very well indeed. As a detective, he used this art in the performance of his duties. He could be harsh, gentle, a perfect listener or an inspired orator – according to the situation. Now he was rather like a father whose son has got into some kind of trouble.

He concentrated on Court. 'You're in a mess,' he told him. 'Your only chance is to be frank with me . . .' And so on. This went on for several hours, with Court sitting sullenly in front of him and refusing to answer – while Mrs Court and Raoul performed the role of reluctant spectators.

But Vidocq was an experienced interrogator – and one, moreover, who had himself been questioned in the past. This gave him an understanding of his subject's mind. He knew, from personal experience, which questions hurt the most: when to become angry, and when to seem to be the gentle friend, the thoroughly good chum in whom everybody confided.

Round about dawn, Court's resistance broke down. 'You really think it would be better if I confessed?' he asked.

'I'm sure it would,' Vidocq assured him. And wondered to himself what the confession would be. He was now convinced that he was guilty of the attack on Fontaine, but there were other crimes to be considered. Throughout his cross-examination, he had been careful never to be too specific.

Much to Vidocq's satisfaction, Court never mentioned the butcher. He simply said: 'It was I who murdered the travelling poultry dealer. I'll tell you, M. Jules, how the thing happened, and I wish I may die if I tell a lie about it.'

For the time being, there was nothing more to be said.

The case rested in the hands of the authorities at Corbeil. The two men were to go before the examining magistrate in that town. While Vidocq was arranging a carriage, Raoul, who seemed to be unmoved by his friend's confession, asked for a pack of cards. When the vehicle was ready, he and his accomplice were engaged in a game of piquet. On the journey out to Corbeil, they fell asleep and did not wake up again until they reached the magistrate's court. It was, Vidocq decided, as if neither man had anything on his conscience.

If Court had already purged himself through confession, it was now Raoul's turn. When they were in front of the magistrate, he gave an almost too convincing demonstration of what had happened to Fontaine. He explained how Court had bludgeoned him, but the blow had only stunned him for a moment. To finish the man off, he – Raoul – had gone for him with a knife. To show what he meant, he picked up a paper knife which was on the magistrate's desk. For a moment, that learned gentleman seemed to think that an attempt was about to be made on his life. But Vidocq gently disarmed the wine merchant.

'Thank you, M. Jules,' Raoul said.

Fontaine, the butcher, was called to identify them. He did so without hesitation. 'Take those murderers from my sight,' he shrieked. 'Their countenances and voices are all too familiar to me.'

It was the last piece of evidence needed. The picture was complete – or nearly. But Vidocq was still not entirely happy. Conceivably only two men were responsible for the attack on Fontaine, but there were the other crimes. Some of them must have needed more than two people. There had to be three, or even four, involved in this small gang.

Again, Vidocq the actor came onto the scene. This time, he was gentle, kindly, almost sympathetic. He told Court and Raoul that they were not bad men by nature. A little bit weak, perhaps, but certainly not evil. Somebody had led them astray.

'I *know* this,' Vidocq told them. 'People have told me so. Some, who will testify against you, have mentioned four people. What do you say to that?'

'That they were wrong,' Raoul said. 'I give you my word of honour that there were never more than three.'

'Three?'

'Yes – three. The other one is a former customs officer. His name is Pons Gérard. You'll find him on the Belgium frontier, in a village there.'

And Raoul warned that he was a powerful man who was always extremely alert. 'If you surprise him,' he said, 'he will put up a desperate resistance, so try if you can to take him asleep.' It was not the first time that a crook had been concerned for this friendly detective's safety.

This assignment, Vidocq decided, called for one of his disguises. He would go as a horse dealer and his two assistants would travel as his grooms. Armed with a good description of Pons Gérard, the three men set off for the Belgian frontier.

It was a rough trip, as there had been a heavy fall of snow. Eventually, after nearly twenty-four hours on the road, they reached a place named La Capelle. They booked rooms at a hotel, and then walked round the town, making inquiries about their prey.

Yes, people agreed, Gérard was a wicked man. Certainly he was a robber, but he was more than that. He was a bully. He had intimidated the local authorities. They knew all about his crimes, but nobody dared to arrest him. Keep out of his way, they warned.

'I understand,' the detective said. 'But, even so, I'd like to meet him. Where does he usually go?'

They mentioned the name of a small inn out in the country. Apparently, it was a haunt of smugglers, and Pons Gérard was one of its best customers.

After breakfast on the following morning, Vidocq and his assistants set off to find it. It had been carefully described to them, and they had no difficulty in reaching the place in time for lunch.

An elderly woman seemed to run the place. She looked tired and made no effort to make them feel welcome. When Vidocq mentioned that he was a friend of Pons Gérard, however, she became more amiable. She brought them some food and they were just about to begin, when a small girl came in.

'You were talking of Gérard,' the landlady said. 'Here's his daughter.'

Vidocq went up to the child and smiled at her. He asked her how her parents were, and then he offered her a reward.

'What do I have to do?' the little girl asked.

'I'm very anxious to meet your mother,' Vidocq told her. 'Will you take me to her?'

The child agreed, and pointed out that she would have done that for nothing.

They walked up the road until they were out of sight of the inn. Then Vidocq said, as if the thought had suddenly occurred to him: 'Tell me – where's your father working these days?'

She pointed down a side road. 'Just down there,' she said.

'Then I'll tell you what we'll do. You run home and tell your mother that you have met three friends of your father, and that we'd like to have supper with him. That will give her time to prepare for us. While you're doing that, we'll go and say "hallo" to him. Isn't that a good idea?'

The little girl said that it was. She ran off. Vidocq and his assistants walked off down the side road. They had not gone very far, when they met a farmworker.

'Do you know where Pons Gérard is?' Vidocq asked.

The man pointed ahead. 'He's with a gang of thirty men, carrying out repairs.'

It seemed that their man was the overseer of the gang. Were the other workers loyal to him? Would they help the detectives, or would they turn against them? Vidocq told the others to wait on the edge of the group while he walked up to the man whom he had identified as the criminal. His face had a friendly smile on it.

'My dear Pons,' he exclaimed – holding out his hand. 'How are you? How's your wife and family? Well, I trust? May I introduce my two grooms to you?' He beckoned to his assistants.

The powerful overseer looked at him for a minute or two in surprise. 'I'm sorry,' he said. 'I don't know who you are.'

Vidocq leaned forward and lowered his voice. 'Yes you do,' he said. 'I am a friend of Raoul and Court. They sent me to you.'

Pons Gérard's face burst into a grin. He held out his massive hand and shook Vidocq's. Although he was only of medium height, it seemed as if the reports about his strength had not been exaggerated. His arms and legs were massive: he wore a large beard and his face, which was brown from almost constant exposure to the sun and the wind, had a curiously determined expression on it. When he was serious, Pons Gérard could obviously be deadly. But now he was delighted at meeting this friend of his associates, and he insisted that they should all take wine together.

'I know of a good place,' he said. 'It's over a mile away, but you won't find a better bottle of wine in this part of France.'

It turned out to be the home of a clockmaker. The wine, as Gérard had promised, was excellent. As they were drinking it, Vidocq steered the conversation round to Raoul and Court.

'Poor fellows,' the detective said, 'I'm afraid they have been arrested. They are now in prison.'

Pons Gérard looked flabbergasted. 'Who arrested them?' he asked.

'Vidocq,' the detective answered.

'That scoundrel! Who is this man of whom we've heard so much? I'd cheerfully give half a dozen bottles of wine to anybody who could bring him to me.'

'There's no need,' the detective said. 'Here I am – and I arrest you.' As the two other detectives handcuffed him, the strong man of the neighbourhood, the robber, the smuggler, the man who had intimidated the local police, sat perfectly still – too astonished to do anything.

Pons Gérard was lucky. He was sentenced to life imprisonment. Court and Raoul were found guilty of the poultry dealer's murder, and were condemned to be executed. It was typical of Vidocq's relationship with criminals, that Court asked for him to be present when he went to the scaffold. They feared Vidocq – at times they hated him, but never for long. Deep in their hearts, the criminals whom he hunted down loved him. They recognized that he had his job to do, and that he never bore a grudge. And the surprising thing was, neither did they.

THREE

DEATH ON THE RAILWAY

It was a summer's evening in 1864. Thomas Briggs had been having an early dinner with his niece and her husband in Peckham. He was sixty-nine: a neat, careful old man who, for all his working life, had been employed by a firm of bankers in the City. Now he was chief clerk, and he enjoyed his responsibilities. Mr Roberts, one of the partners, used to say that the firm would fall to pieces without Briggs. Thomas Briggs always laughed at this remark, but he liked it. In many ways, he believed it was true.

It was not yet dark as he stood up and looked at his gold watch. 'Eight o'clock, my dears,' he said. 'I'd best be going.' His niece's husband, whose name was Buchan, remembered the watch vividly. It had two keys tied on to the chain by a piece of string. The string seemed out of place.

'I'll walk with you to the bus stop,' he said.

Mr Briggs picked up his hat, the stick with a heavy handle that he always carried with him, and a black leather bag which contained some business papers.

'You've plenty of time, uncle,' the niece said.

The old man smiled. 'And a good thing,' he said. 'One doesn't like to hurry at my age.'

It was only a short walk to the bus stop in the Old Kent Road. The evening was almost oppressively warm, and Buchan wondered whether it was going to thunder.

They had a few minutes to wait. The stop was outside a public house called the Lord Nelson, and they could hear people singing inside. Mr Briggs remarked that they seemed to be very happy.

'It's Saturday night,' Buchan said – as if that explained everything.

Presently the horse bus arrived. Mr Briggs wished Buchan a good night; climbed on board; and bought a ticket to King William Street. From there he walked to Fenchurch Street Station, where he bought a first-class ticket to Hackney Wick. The inspector at the entrance to the platform did not remember him afterwards, but that was not surprising. The trains were running five minutes' late that night and he was unusually busy.

Mr Briggs walked down to the front of the train. He found an empty compartment nearest to the engine. He put his hat, his stick, and his bag on the rack, and settled down in the corner. At 9.50, the train pulled slowly out of the station.

Two of Mr Briggs' younger colleagues from the bank, Harry Verney and Sidney Jones, happened to get onto the same train that night. They joined it at Hackney Wick, the station at which the old man had intended to alight. By a strange coincidence, they climbed into the compartment nearest to the engine. It was already empty.

They had just sat down, when Sidney Jones noticed that the seat was wet. 'What do you make of this, Harry?' he asked. His trousers now had a large patch of red on them. 'Wouldn't you say this was blood?' he said.

Verney agreed that it certainly looked like it, and pointed to the door. 'Look – there's some more of it there,' he said. 'Don't you think we should call the guard?'

The guard was just about to send the train on the next stage of its journey, when the two young men told him what they had seen. At first he was sceptical. How, he wanted to know, would blood get into a railway compartment? But Verney and Jones were insistent, and he agreed to have a look.

Calling out to the engine driver that they 'wouldn't be a minute', he walked with the young men to the front of the train. It was getting dark now, and the compartment wasn't very well lit. Nevertheless, as the guard reported afterwards, there was no mistaking the fact that there was blood there – and, what was more, a good deal of it. Up on the luggage rack, he found a hat and the black bag in which Mr Briggs carried his documents. Under one of the seats, there was a stick with a heavy handle. The end of it, like the seat and the door, was covered with blood.

'I'm sorry, gentlemen,' the guard said. 'This train will not be going your way. You'll have to catch the next one. I'll have to lock this compartment up.'

The other passengers were called out onto the platform. The guard locked the carriage, and the train went off to the sidings at Chalk Farm. The next people to board it would be the police.

Meanwhile, a train of empty carriages had been travelling from Hackney Wick to Bow. At one point, the track went over a bridge which crossed a canal. On the far side, the driver suddenly put on the brakes. Once they had come to a halt, the guard came up to the front. The driver, he noticed, was climbing down from his cab.

'What's the trouble?' he asked.

'We just passed something beside the track,' the driver said. 'It looked as if it might be a body. I thought we ought to investigate.'

They walked back over the bridge and there, sure enough, lay the figure of an old man. He was still breathing but the side of his head was a nasty mess and he was unconscious.

'Look,' the guard said. 'There's a pub down there in the street. The Mitford Castle. Why don't we take the poor old fellow there?'

They carried him carefully down the embankment and into the bar. One of the staff was sent to fetch a doctor. Presently, he came back with a surgeon named Francis Toulmin. Mr Toulmin looked at the injured man, and then exclaimed: 'Good grief! It's one of my own patients.'

'You know him?' the landlord asked.

'Of course I do – it's Thomas Briggs. Have you sent for the police?'

'They're coming round. Do you think he'll live?'

'I shall do all that I can,' Mr Toulmin said. 'I can't hold out many hopes, though. He's an old man and somebody has hit him very hard about the head.'

Mr Thomas Briggs was taken to his home at Clapton Square near Hackney. On the following evening, he died. The poor old man never regained consciousness.

Inspector Kerressey of 'K' Division was in charge of the case. He had got in touch with Mr Briggs' son, who identified the bag and the stick as his father's. The hat, he said, did not belong to him. Mr Briggs Senior, he explained, always liked to wear hats with a rather tall crown. 'Bell crowns', he believed they called them. He got them from a firm in the city. The hat in the compartment was about 1½ inches shorter than his father's. What was more, it had a very distinctive striped lining.

The victim's gold watch and chain had been stolen; but, surprisingly, nothing else. He had been wearing a diamond ring, and it was still on his finger. Four gold sovereigns were still in his trouser-pocket, and a silver snuff box was in another pocket. Nor had the bag on the luggage rack been tampered with.

According to Mr Toulmin, somebody had hit Mr Briggs four times in the area of the left ear with a blunt instrument. The blows had been hard ones. The walking stick, which the guard had found under the seat, had probably been used. There was no need to look much farther for a weapon.

For the rest, there was little to go on. The ticket inspector could not remember who had got on the train, and nor could the railway officials at other stations down the line. Since the carriage did not have a corridor, and this was in the days before communication cords were introduced, Mr Briggs would have been helpless.

So: somebody had got into the compartment and somewhere between Bow and Hackney, he had struck the old man over the head with his own stick. He had wrenched the gold watch out of his waistcoat pocket, and then had thrown his victim out onto the line. After that, he had made his own getaway. But he had made one mistake. In the heat of the moment, he had taken Mr Briggs' hat instead of his own.

Could they find the owner of this hat? A label inside showed that it had been sold by a firm named H. Walker of 40 Crawford Street, W1. It was just off Baker Street.

Inspector Kerressey went round there and saw Mr Walker.

Yes, Mr Walker agreed, this was one of his firm's hats. 'A very popular one,' he said. 'Some gentlemen prefer the rather more shallow crown. We sell a good many of them.'

Could Mr Walker remember anybody in particular who had purchased one?

Mr Walker smiled apologetically. He was sorry. They had so many customers. One really could not remember them all.

But, Inspector Kerressey pointed out, this one had a rather unusual lining.

'All our hats do,' Mr Walker said patiently. 'We like to think that they are just as smart on the inside as they are on the outside.'

As Inspector Kerressey made his way back to the police station, he felt depressed. The trail had suddenly gone cold. The hat had been his one great hope. Now it seemed to be useless.

The newspapers had much to say about the killing and, on the Monday, three rewards were offered for information. The Government promised £100, the bank which had employed Mr Briggs promised £100, and so did the railway company. The hooks, as you might say, had been baited. All they could do now was wait.

On the Tuesday morning, the police had their first response. A cab driver named Matthews came round to the police station. He wished, he said, to speak to an officer. It was about the murder of Thomas Briggs.

Inspector Kerressey hurried out to the counter. What did Mr Matthews have to tell him? he asked.

It was about the hat, Matthews said. He, too, had one just like it. It had been greatly admired by a young

German – fellow by the name of Müller. He was a tailor – used to work for a friend of his. This chap Müller came round to his house occasionally. One day, he had struck a deal with Matthews. If he would buy him a hat just like his own, he, Müller, would make him a waistcoat. It had seemed a pretty fair exchange, and Matthews had gone round to Walker's. The hat, he remembered, had cost fourteen shillings.

'This man – Müller,' Kerressey said. 'Does he come round to your house frequently?'

'Now and again,' Matthews said. 'As a matter of fact, he was there yesterday. That was what made me think of this business. He gave my young daughter a box. You know – something for her to play with. The thing was that it had an unusual name on it. "Death". That's an odd name, don't you think?'

Inspector Kerressey agreed that it was. 'Where could I see this box?' he asked.

'I've got it with me,' Matthews said. 'It's only a small thing. Sort of thing you might pack up a watch and chain in. As a matter of fact, I remember that it did come from a jeweller's. Here . . .'

He felt in his pocket and pulled out a small, brown, cardboard box. On the lid was printed the name 'Death' – a firm which, apparently, had premises in Cheapside.

'Did I do right in coming round?' Matthews asked.

Inspector Kerressey assured him that he had done right.

The firm named Death turned out to be a business which combined the sale of watches and jewellery with pawnbroking. The proprietor himself remembered serving a young man who spoke with a German accent. It had been on the Monday, he recalled.

Did he know what the man's name was? He was not sure. If the inspector would excuse him for a moment ... Mr Death went to a small room at the back of the shop, where he spoke to one of his assistants.

When he returned, he asked the Inspector: 'Has this to do with the murder of Mr Briggs?'

Kerressey said that it had. 'Ah yes,' said Mr Death. 'I thought perhaps that was the case. In fact, we had two visits from the young gentleman you are talking about. The first occasion was some weeks ago.'

His name, it seemed, was Franz Müller. He had called on the first occasion to pawn his watch and chain. They had not been worth very much. He had been given £2 for the watch and £1 for the chain.

The second time, he had a gold watch chain with him. It was quite a good one, and Mr Death had been able to offer him £3 10s for it. Müller redeemed his own watch and chain and spent the balance of five shillings (there was five shillings commission for Mr Death) on a ring.

Did he know where Franz Müller lived? Mr Death was sorry – he did not. Could Inspector Kerressey see the chain which had been pawned? It was brought out from one of the drawers. Two keys were tied onto it by a piece of string. There could be little doubt about who its rightful owner had been.

It was tantalizing. They seemed to be so near to finding the solution to the case, and yet it was still out of reach. They knew where this man Müller's hat had been bought. They knew where he had pawned Mr Briggs' watch chain. They had even met a friend of his, but nobody seemed to know where he lived. If all the police forces in London were mobilized, it would take them weeks to trudge from door to door, asking whether

a young German named Franz Müller lived there.
And, by then, he might have changed his name – or,
even, gone back to his native country.

The newspapers were still giving prominence to the
case, and placards announcing the reward were well dis-
played. But, since the visit of the cab driver Matthews,
nobody had come forward. It was almost as if there was
a conspiracy of silence against the police.

Inspector Kerressey went round to Matthews' house.
The atmosphere was strained, and they seemed to feel
uncomfortable in the police officer's presence. It was
almost as if they, themselves, felt guilty. Could they tell
the Inspector anything more about Franz Müller. Mr
Matthews thought about it. 'Only that I loaned him
seven shillings and sixpence the other day,' he said. 'I
don't suppose that's important,' he added apologetically.

It might be, the Inspector said. One never knew. 'You
say he worked for one of your friends,' he said.
'Wouldn't he know where he lived?'

Mr Matthews said that it had been some time ago. He
believed that he had moved his lodgings since then.

'Think very carefully,' the Inspector said. 'Didn't he
say anything at all – even about what district it was? He
must have told you *something*.'

There was a minute or two's silence. Then Mrs Matthews said: 'Do you know – I think it was somewhere in
North London.'

Inspector Kerressey thanked her. It was, he supposed, of some help. But there was a great deal of North
London.

It was Friday. In spite of the reward, no more information had turned up. Inspector Kerressey was almost beginning to believe that this man Franz Müller did not exist. 'North London!' he exclaimed to the sergeant who was working with him. 'How many people do you suppose live there?'

The sergeant said that he had no idea, but it must be a good many. 'But, sir,' he observed, 'it might be possible to narrow it down a little bit more than this. The crime was committed between Bow and Hackney Wick stations. Is this not, perhaps, significant?'

'Possibly,' the Inspector grunted.

He was wondering whether he could make anything of this, when a message came for him. It seemed that a German named Repsch had called at a police station in the City. He had some information about the Briggs case. If Inspector Kerressey would care to visit him . . .

The sun was blazing down as the Inspector turned off Moorgate into Old Jewry where Mr and Mrs Repsch lived. The threatened storm of nearly a week ago had eventually moved off towards the west and a heat wave had followed it. The Inspector thought sympathetically of all the clerks crammed inside City offices. In this weather, it must be like working in an oven.

He found the German couple living in a large room on the first floor of an old building. In spite of the fact that Repsch seemed to take in humble tailoring jobs for a living, the premises were spotlessly clean. Mrs Repsch smiled easily, and asked the Inspector whether he would like a cup of chocolate. He thanked her, and asked whether he might have a glass of water instead. It was too warm for hot drinks.

Mr Repsch was the more serious of the two. One

might have imagined that he was prone to worrying – even when things were going well. At the moment, he looked extremely upset.

'It is about young Franz,' he said. 'Do you really think he killed this man?'

The Inspector said that they had no proof as yet, but it certainly seemed likely.

'I am sorry,' Mr Repsch said. 'I should have gone to the police station before. I did not know what to do. You see Franz Müller is a great friend of ours. It did not seem possible that he could have hurt anybody.'

Bit by bit, Inspector Kerressey was able to piece together the story. It seemed that Müller had come to England from Saxe Coburg in Germany two years earlier. His first job had been with a firm of tailors. After a short time, the proprietor had told him that he could no longer afford to employ him. Müller had moved on. In a fairly short space of time, he had worked at three places, but each of them had been compelled to get rid of him. His last job had been with a gentleman named Hodgkinson in Threadneedle Street near the Bank of England.

'It wasn't that Franz was bad at his work,' Mr Repsch explained. 'You know how it is. Times become hard. Somebody has to go.'

After leaving Mr Hodgkinson, he had been out of work for several weeks. Things had become so bad that he had decided to go to America. It was, of course, a gamble but his experiences in London had taught him not to expect very much.

But still there was trouble. The fare to the United States in those days was £4. Müller had already pawned his watch and chain, and he had not enough money. The Repschs had loaned him 10s 6d towards the passage, but that was nothing like sufficient.

'And then, you know, he seemed to come into some money,' Mr Repsch said. 'When he came to see us on Monday, he was wearing a new hat. The crown was much taller than his usual one. He also had a new watch. It was a very nice one: much better than the one he had pawned.

'My wife teased him. "Franz," she said, "you have been extravagant. How will you get to America like this?" But he said that he had been able to buy the hat for very little, and he had bought the watch from a sailor down at the docks.'

Kerressey fished inside a box which he had brought with him. Out of it he took the hat which had been found in the railway compartment.

'Would you recognize this?' he asked.

'Ya, ya. That is Franz's,' Mr Repsch said. 'Do you see the brim? It is curled up a little bit at one side. Franz used to like to wear it like that; he thought it made him look more handsome. He always used to have this hat with him. He used to keep his letters tucked into the band. That is funny, isn't it?'

'He was here on Monday,' Kerressey said. 'When did you see him before that?'

'On the Saturday. He left here between seven and eight o'clock in the evening. He was going to see a girl-friend, I think.'

'Would he have called at his lodgings on the way?'

'It is possible. I know he was going to Fenchurch Street Station. That was where he caught the train to Hackney Wick.'

'Hackney Wick?' echoed the Inspector. 'Is that where he lived?'

'Didn't you know? He had lodgings at Victoria Park,

near Hackney Wick station. His landlady was called Mrs Blyth, I think.'

On his way back to the police station, the Inspector called at Mrs Blyth's house. It was a neat, semi-detached villa, with trees lining the street outside. Mrs Blyth was a friendly woman who seemed quite unworried by a visit from a police officer.

'How can I help you, Inspector?' she asked.

'You have a lodger named Müller?'

'Franz Müller. Yes – that's right. His room was on the first floor – at the back.'

'You say his room *was* at the back. Has he gone away?'

'Oh yes – didn't you know? He's gone to America. I forget when his ship sailed – yesterday, I believe. A sailing ship called the *Victoria*. I think that was the one.'

Perhaps it was the hot weather: possibly it was the frustration of the case. Inspector Kerressey felt that he was about to become irritable.

'Mrs Blyth,' he said with all the patience that he could find, 'do you not realize that we want Müller in connexion with a murder?'

Her good-natured housewife's face dropped an inch or two at this. 'Murder!' she exclaimed. 'You can't mean that. Franz Müller wanted for killing somebody? It's impossible.'

'I'm afraid it isn't, Mrs Blyth,' the Inspector said. 'Did he come back here on Saturday night? That was the ninth, in case you have forgotten.'

'Saturday? Yes – I heard him come in. It was after eleven o'clock, I remember that. I'd gone to bed by then, but I distinctly heard him.'

'And on the Sunday? What did he do then?'

Mrs Blyth said that he had spent most of the day indoors. In the afternoon, he had taken a short walk with herself and her husband. Otherwise, it had been an uneventful day.

The Inspector asked whether he had seemed to be in any way different: whether, for example, he might have had something on his mind.

'He always had something on his mind,' Mrs Blyth said. 'Leastways during the past few weeks. He was unemployed, you know – and he became very short of cash. Sometimes, he had a job to pay the rent. But he was always very correct. He used to let me have it as regular as clockwork – never owed me anything.'

But, *on the Sunday*? No, Mrs Blyth said, he was much the same as usual. There was only one thing which puzzled her: how had he found the cash to go to America when he was always so hard up?

Back at the police station, Kerressey found that his sergeant was waiting for him. The man looked exhausted, as well he might. He had spent the day in the City, travelling from one pawnbroker's shop to another.

'I never knew there were so many of them,' he said.

'Did you have any luck?' the Inspector asked.

The sergeant gave him a package. 'Look in there,' he said.

Kerressey unwrapped it and found a watch and chain. 'Müller's?' he asked.

'Yes. He pawned them on Monday at a shop belonging to a fellow named Cox.'

'How much did he get for them?'

'The same as the other chap gave him: two pounds for the watch and one pound for the chain.'

How did the story look now? It was fair to assume, Kerressey told the sergeant, that Müller had been with the Repschs until about eight o'clock on the Saturday. He had then walked to Fenchurch Street and caught the 9.45 train, which was running five minutes' late. Or had he? There was a gap of over an hour to fill in. Could he have gone to see his girlfriend and *then* caught the train?

But – assume that he did catch the 9.45. Since nobody was checking the tickets, it was reasonable to believe that he entered a first-class carriage with a second-class ticket. It was illegal, but Müller wouldn't have been the first to commit such an offence – nor the last.

He had found himself alone in the compartment with an old gentleman who was wearing a handsome gold watch. That watch would raise sufficient money to pay his fare across the Atlantic. He decided to steal it.

Possibly Mr Briggs fell asleep as the train left Fenchurch Street. Müller may have tried to take the watch from him by stealth; but, in doing so, he woke him up. Seeing a stick on the luggage rack, he hit the old man with it. Possibly he had only intended to knock him unconscious. But why had he hit him four times – and so hard? From the accounts of people who had known him, the young German didn't seem the type to indulge in unnecessary violence.

Perhaps he thought that Mr Briggs was already dead when he pushed him off the train. Did he, himself, jump off at the same time? And how was one to account for the time gap between the crime and his return home to Victoria Park? Was it *then* that he went to see the girl?

Monday was easier to account for. At ten o'clock, he had gone to Mr Death's premises, where he had pawned Mr Briggs' watch chain. He had redeemed his own watch and chain with the money, and accepted a cheap ring to make up the difference. Then he had gone to another pawnbroker's, Mr Cox's, where he had once again put his own watch and chain in pawn. The result of all these somewhat complicated transactions was that Müller was now £3 better off. Add to this the 7s 6d he had borrowed from Matthews and the 10s 6d Repsch had loaned him, and he had almost enough money to buy a ticket to America. It was reasonable to suppose that he already had the balance of the fare.

But, as Kerressey said, there were still rather a lot of holes. The only person who could complete the story was Müller and he, from his landlady's account, was on his way across the Atlantic in a sailing ship named the *Victoria*.

'There's only one thing to be done,' said the Inspector. 'We shall have to go to New York. Furthermore, we shall have to get there ahead of Müller.'

'How can that be done?' the sergeant asked.

'Go by steamship. I just hope that there is a sailing within the next few days.'

There was – in a steamer named the *Etna*.

Inspector Kerressey was one of the people waiting on the quayside at New York when the *Victoria* docked. When Müller was pointed out to him by the captain, he received something of a surprise. His conversations with Mr Matthews, Mr and Mrs Repsch and Mrs Blyth should have prepared him for somebody who was a good way removed from the traditional villain, and they were right. He was shortish, slightly built, and had light-brown hair. He was dressed in a brown morning coat, and he looked almost boyish compared to the older passengers.

T–C

When the Inspector told him that he had come to arrest him for the murder of Thomas Briggs, he flatly denied it. Unfortunately for the young German, the evidence which was to hang him was on his head, and sewn up in a canvas bag in his valise. The former was his hat: the latter, a watch which Mr Briggs' son identified as his father's.

Inspector Kerressey's most important task was to bring Müller back to England. The American authorities made no difficulty about an extradition warrant; and, when the *Etna* made her return trip, the detective and the young man accused of murder went with her.

They never succeeded in filling in the time gaps of the Saturday. Müller's girlfriend was a young lady named Ann Eldred, and she swore that he had spent the whole evening with her. But the silent evidence of the hat was more damning than a thousand alibis.

The name inside the crown was Dignance & Co, Royal Exchange, London. Inspector Kerressey took it round to the hatters and asked them to examine it. At first, they said that it was not one of theirs: the crown was too low. But they could not deny the label, and they looked at it more carefully.

Presently, the manager of the firm said that it had been altered. 'One and a half inches has been taken off the crown,' he said. He pointed out that the modification had not been done by an experienced hatter. In this case, he explained, the work would have been executed with a flat iron and varnish. Instead, the crown had been neatly stitched back into place – just as a tailor might have done it.

Was there any evidence to show that the hat had once belonged to Mr Briggs? The manager said that the place where customers' names were printed had been re-

*. . . a man who had been killed for the sake of a
gold watch and chain*

moved. This, presumably, was why the crown had been shortened.

'But,' he said, 'there was an unusual feature to Mr Briggs' last hat. When he came to try it on, he complained that it was a little bit large for his liking. We said that we could do something about that immediately, and one of my assistants stuffed some silver paper in the lining. It worked very well.'

'You mean,' Inspector Kerressey said, 'that if you can find some silver paper in the lining of this hat, you will be prepared to identify it as the one you sold to Mr Briggs?'

'Precisely.'

'Then please look.'

The manager turned the hat over, felt underneath the lining, and pulled out a length of silver paper.

'You see, Inspector?' he said.

They hanged Franz Müller in November. He was twenty-four years old. He never admitted that he had murdered Thomas Briggs. The jury at his trial, on the other hand, only took twenty-five minutes to decide that he was guilty. Afterwards, the judge told them that he agreed with their verdict.

Because of his crime, the railways of Britain became a safer means of transport. The corridor coach had not yet been invented, and there was no means of sending out distress signals for people who were sealed off from the world in compartments. Within a year or so of Thomas Briggs' murder, the communications cord was introduced. But it arrived too late to save this poor old man who had been killed for the sake of a gold watch and chain.

FOUR

PORTRAITS ON THE FURNITURE

The nineteenth-century detectives caught their men the hard way. They observed, they interrogated, they plodded from one suspect to another. There were no short cuts. Science, which is the ally of present-day investigators, had little to offer them.

Had they but known it, there were scraps of valuable knowledge available. If only somebody could have put them together, the work of the police would have been much easier. For example, the early Chinese had discovered that people's fingers have distinctive markings on them – complex patterns of minute ridges, which never repeat themselves.

They used them as a way of identifying documents. When a man pressed his thumb onto a seal, the impression it left behind was as binding as a signature. It was extremely useful in a country where only a small number of citizens could read or write.

In Europe a doctor named Jean-Evangeliste Purkinje carried out research into fingerprints in the year 1819. Unfortunately, it never occurred to him that it had any practical application. If he had persevered, he would probably have discovered a means of identifying criminals. But the doctor's interest drifted towards something else, and he left the project unfinished.

Nevertheless he had established that, whenever a human hand touches anything, it leaves a mark. It cannot always be seen; but if the object is brushed over with white powder (such as French chalk) the latent fingerprints immediately appear.

This would not mean very much if people's fingers were identical. Luckily for detectives, they are not. When the subject was re-examined at the end of the nineteenth century, one of the criminologists concerned was Francis Galton. As well as being a scientist, Galton was a brilliant statistician. He calculated that the chances of two people having the same prints are 64,000 million to one against.

Galton's discovery was the kind of break-through that detectives had been hoping for. A suspect might deny that he was present at a certain place; but if his fingerprints were found there, his alibi was smashed. In his war against the police, the criminal could make sure that he left no traces by wearing gloves. But, in a surprisingly large number of cases, this precaution was overlooked.

With the odds that Francis Galton worked out, it is obvious that fingerprints can never tell a direct lie. There was one occasion, however, when they misled the police. Indeed, they were responsible for detectives in Paris spending a great many wasted days – looking for a character who never existed.

During the summer of 1910 a series of jewel robberies took place in the French capital. They were brilliantly executed, and the pattern of each was the same. They were always committed at night, and the thieves seemed to take great care to pick a victim who lived on his own. When he went to bed, everything was in perfect order. But when he woke up, the front door had been forced open: his safe had been opened and his most valuable possessions removed. With so much activity going on, one might have imagined that the intruders would have disturbed their victims. But no: without exception, they had all slept soundly on in spite of the noise.

The police were baffled by it. If there had been a servant or somebody else living on the premises, they might have imagined that the householder had been drugged. As it was, this profound ability to sleep through the crime seemed inexplicable.

At eight o'clock one morning towards the end of the summer, the police received a telephone call from the Count de Commercy. The story he told them was becoming sadly familiar: he lived in an expensive part of Paris and he had been robbed of some valuable heirlooms. Within fifteen minutes, detectives were at his front door. It was half open, and they saw that it had been forced by a jemmy.

The Count, who was still wearing his pyjamas under an elegant silk dressing-gown, came into the hall to greet them.

'Good morning, gentlemen,' he said.

There were four detectives in all. The Superintendent, his assistant, a fingerprint expert, and a photographer. They noticed that a tall vase on a table by one of the windows had been broken. Otherwise, nothing had been disturbed except in the Count's study. The safe had been burnt open by an acetylene torch, and some of the contents were lying on the carpet. These were mainly documents. All the valuable items had been removed.

While the fingerprint expert was dusting over the furniture with French chalk, the Superintendent questioned the Count.

'I noticed that you seem to be alone here,' he said. 'Do you not employ any servants?'

The Count said that he had a housekeeper who came during the daytime. Her job was to keep the place clean and to prepare his lunch. She would be arriving at half past eight.

'Your dinner in the evening?' the Superintendent said. 'Does she cook that, too?'

'No,' the Count said. 'I nearly always dine out.'

'And last night?'

'I dined at a restaurant with some friends.'

The detective fingered his watch chain uncomfortably. 'You'll forgive me for asking this question, I hope,' he said. 'But, you understand – I have to. Did you have much to drink yesterday evening?'

'I drink very little. Yesterday, I did not take more than I normally do.'

'And yet you did not notice that the crime had been committed until this morning. You are sure that nobody could have come in while you were out at dinner?'

'Quite sure,' the Count said. 'I went into my study before going to bed. The safe was intact. Besides – I'd have noticed if the front door had been forced.'

'Yes – of course you would.' The Superintendent got up from his chair and walked over to the fire place. The same old pattern was beginning to appear. A person living on his own. The crime committed at night. The thieves seeming to have the run of the flat without disturbing the occupant.

'Please tell me,' he said, 'are you normally a heavy sleeper?'

'That is the strange thing. No – I'm a light sleeper. But last night I dropped off within about half an hour of going to bed. And I slept very deeply. Usually I wake up at about half past six. Today, it was eight o'clock. When I woke up, I had a slight headache and an unpleasant taste in my mouth.'

The Count smiled. 'But I promise you, Super-intendent – I had no more than half a bottle of wine and a cognac to drink.'

'You are suggesting that you were drugged?' the Superintendent asked.

'Yes – it was like that. But I can't see how.'

'Did you have anything to drink when you came home? Anything at all?'

'Just a glass of water,' the Count said. 'I always drink one before putting out my light. I keep a jug on my bedside table.'

'One last question, sir. When you were out, did you leave any windows open?'

'I see what you're getting at,' the Count said. 'As a matter of fact – I did. My bedroom window. I like plenty of fresh air, and it was warm yesterday. You think that somebody may have climbed in through it, and put a drug into my drinking water?'

'One has to admit the possibility,' the Superintendent said.

'Then – if I may show you, I think I can settle this point.'

The two men walked into the bedroom and over to the window. The Count's apartment was on the fourth floor. A sheer drop of nearly fifty feet lay between the window and the street.

'How would you like to climb up that?' the Count asked.

The Inspector agreed that it seemed to be impossible.

By now, the fingerprint man had finished his work. He was talking to the housekeeper who had arrived, and was looking at the mess of French chalk with a good deal of disapproval. He produced two pieces of wax from his bag.

'You've photographed the prints?' the Superintendent asked.

'Yes.'

'Very well. Now sir (turning to the Count), if we could just take your fingerprints and those of this lady, we'll be on our way.'

'Is that really necessary?' the Count asked.

The Superintendent said that it was. He pointed out that there were a great many prints in the apartment. If they could establish which belonged to the Count, and which to the housekeeper, anything that remained could be regarded with suspicion. The Count agreed and so, more reluctantly, did the woman.

Some hours later, the Superintendent was in conference with the fingerprint expert. The latter explained that most of the prints tallied with those of the Count and his housekeeper. But another set had been found in the Count's bedroom. They were of a somewhat singular type.

The state of the art was now such that any criminal who was arrested immediately had his prints taken. Unless he wore gloves, all his subsequent movements could be traced. Although those found in the bedroom did not belong to any known villain, they were able to give the detectives a certain amount of information. The size of the hand which had made them indicated that they belonged to a child – probably a boy. Furthermore, the experience of an earlier case suggested that he belonged to a 'criminal and degenerate type.'

For the next week or two, the crime squad visited the haunts of the city's underworld. They were looking for a gang who employed a young boy who had never been arrested, and who was unusually agile. The Superintendent still believed that it would have been impossible for any human being to climb, even up a drainpipe, into the Count's bedroom. But it was all they had to go on.

And the search drew a blank. The citizens of the Paris underworld had children: sometimes they used youngsters in their schemes, but none of them would have been able to make the ascent up the side of the building.

Nevertheless, an analysis of the water in the jug on the Count's bedside table had showed that it had contained a drug. The chemist explained that the Count would have become unconscious within forty-five minutes of drinking it, and that it would have caused him to sleep unusually heavily.

'A squadron of cavalry could have galloped through the apartment, and he would not have heard it,' the chemist said.

How had it been administered? It had probably been brought into the apartment in a small bottle. It had then been tipped into the jug. Surely the Count would have noticed an unusual taste? Not necessarily. Was he a heavy smoker? Yes – he smoked cigars. 'There you are, then,' the chemist said. 'Smoking would have taken the edge off his palate. If he drank the water quickly, he could easily have been unaware of anything unusual about it.'

The Superintendent returned to his office and stretched across his desk for a sheet of paper. On it, he wrote:

1. While the Count was at dinner, somebody entered the apartment and put a drug in the water by his bedside.

2. The front door had not been forced at this time. (NOTE: if they had managed to get into the flat to drug the water, why had they bothered to force open the door later on?)

3. Whoever put the drug into the water must have entered the flat through the window – there was no other way in. (Or: *had* they? Could the drug have been administered by the housekeeper before she went off duty. Remember to ask the Count how long the woman has been in his service.)

4. The intruder's fingerprints were found only in the Count's bedroom. Why only there? There MUST be a connexion between these prints and the drug.

More as a formality than anything else, the Superintendent questioned the Count about his housekeeper. She had worked for him for twelve years, and he had never had any reason to mistrust her. One could not, he said, hope for a more loyal servant.

Was she married? Did she have any dubious friends whom she might have admitted to the apartment? She was not married. The Count knew little about her friends, but he assumed that they were as respectable as she was.

And so the investigation continued. At every turn, it seemed to produce far more questions than answers. The Superintendent was beginning to think that he would have to add it to the list of other jewel robberies that had gone unsolved that year. The prospect was not a happy one. It meant that some gang could go on helping themselves to precious stones until they ran out of victims.

It was in this despondent mood that he went to see the department's fingerprint expert again.

'This case is impossible,' he told him. 'No boy could have climbed up the drainpipe and drugged the Count's drinking water. Can't you do better for me than that?'

His companion laughed. 'I could,' he said, 'but I doubt whether it would be of any help.'

'Never mind about that. Anything, and I mean *anything*, would be better than nothing.'

'I told you that there was something unusual about the prints,' the expert said. 'I meant that. They could have belonged to a degenerate boy: they *might* have belonged to a chimpanzee.'

He went on to explain that it was generally believed that most apes had fingerprints which were much more rudimentary than those of human beings. But he had done some research into the subject, and he had discovered that there was a certain species of chimpanzee in which the fingerprints bore a startling resemblance to those of people. The arcs and loops were definitely almost human.

'You are telling me that these prints may not have been made by a boy at all?' the Superintendent said.

'It is possible.'

The Superintendent lit a cigarette thoughtfully. This put an entirely different complexion on things. A boy could not have climbed up the outside of a building, but a chimpanzee might have managed it. Could such an animal have been trained to do this: and, which was just as important, trained to tip a bottle of liquid into a jug? And could it also have been taught to climb back to the street once more, once its work was done?

Surely not. The creature would have had to be unusually intelligent, and somebody would have noticed it. But then he reminded himself that the bedroom was at the back of the building. There was very little lighting on this side.

He now applied himself to trying to remember who, if anyone, among the criminal classes kept a chimpanzee as a pet. He could think of nobody.

The robberies gradually faded into the background, as the Superintendent became involved with other work. Some weeks after the Count de Commercy's jewels had been stolen, he was investigating a murder. The victim was one of a notorious gang of women thieves. She had been killed by a knife with an unusually ornate handle. The evidence suggested that the murderer had thrown it.

Knife-throwing requires a special skill. The police believed the crime had been committed by another member of the gang – a woman of Egyptian nationality who was well known to the authorities. Indeed, she had already spent a certain amount of time in prison. On this occasion, however, there did not seem to be enough evidence to arrest her.

In a final attempt to force a confession out of her, the Superintendent and two of his colleagues had gone round to the woman's house. They were subjecting her to a bombardment of questions, when one of the detectives heard sounds coming from an adjacent room.

'You have a visitor,' he said.

'There is nobody,' the woman replied. 'It is your imagination.'

The superintendent tried to remember who, among the criminal classes, owned a chimpanzee

The Superintendent listened carefully. His colleague had been right. There was somebody in the next room. He walked quickly across and pulled open the door. He was greeted by an amiable chimpanzee.

The woman and the chimpanzee were taken back to police headquarters. The woman, who was considered to be the less interesting of the two, was locked in a cell. The ape was taken to the Superintendent's office.

'Get me a jug and a small bottle of water,' he told one of his assistants. When the detective returned, the jug was put on the desk. 'Now,' said the Superintendent, 'we shall give the bottle to this monkey, and see what happens.'

The creature accepted the small bottle without any hesitation at all. For a second, it seemed to grin at the policemen. Then it bounded across the room and tipped the contents into the jug.

'I think we have found the culprit,' the Superintendent said.

When the animal's fingerprints were taken, they corresponded with those which had been found in the bedroom. On a further examination of the premises, the forensic experts found the remains of lice which are not associated with even the lowest types of human being, but are found on monkeys. If the housekeeper had been more conscientious in her dusting, this portion of the evidence would have been thrown away.

However, one problem remained. There was not enough evidence to convict the Egyptian woman of either the robberies or the murder. The chimpanzee had demonstrated its guilt and there was no longer any doubt about how the crimes had been carried out. But an animal cannot be sent to prison: indeed, it cannot be charged and then tried. What were the police to do?

They both had to be released, but this was the woman's swan song to crime. Shortly afterwards, she was arrested for another offence, and she went to prison for a long, long time.

Author's Note: When compiling this collection of cases I had some doubts about whether to include this story. My fear was that none of my readers would believe it. But it is, I assure you, perfectly true. The case is referred to in *Clues and Crime* which was written by that distinguished criminologist Henry T. F. Rhodes and was published by John Murray in 1933.

FIVE

NO APPLAUSE FOR THE ACTOR

Ever since Sherlock Holmes walked into a novel and became the world's first great fictional detective, the formula for this kind of literature has been more or less unchanged. Villains are given credit for far more intelligence than most of them possess. Policemen are large, lumbering creatures, who plod like patient cows about their duties and seldom come up with any bright thoughts. And, in the foreground, there is Super Sleuth – usually an amateur – who scratches his head and wrinkles his brow, and thinks, and thinks, and thinks. Eventually, when he has thought for long enough, he gathers all the characters together and tells them who did it, how he did it, and why he did it.

It all makes fascinating reading; but it bears more relationship to doing a crossword puzzle than it does to solving a crime in real life. Few criminals are bright enough to weave the tangled plots of these stories. Many of them are youths who hold up poor old postmistresses and rob them of the petty cash. They have already been in Borstal: they have done, as the saying goes, 'a bit of bird'.* Now, they're qualified: they are members of the club. Borstal has left a scar on their minds, and it will take a lot of understanding to remove it. They are ready

* An underground expression for a spell in prison. It refers to 'doing time', which rhyming slang expresses as 'bird-lime', and therefore, 'bird'.

to begin their grown-up lives as professional criminals. If the old lady has a pound or two in the till – well, it's an easy job for a beginner.

As they grow older, their methods improve and they become more ambitious. During their sojourns in prison (for they always get caught), they pick up a few ideas, and they try to apply them. Prison, to a criminal, is what a technical college is to an ambitious young engineer.

The police are by no means a bunch of bumbling bovines, but a highly trained body of men backed up by brilliantly clever scientific equipment. And, as for the Super Sleuth – he does not exist. Crimes are not solved by clever amateurs with agile minds and a happy turn of phrase. They are investigated by a team of men, patiently following up leads, sometimes being disappointed, but, by sheer determination, usually producing the answer.

Not all detectives in fiction, of course, are projected as intellectuals. There is the private eye, for example: a man who occupies a small office, keeps a bottle of whisky in the filing cabinet, and takes a suitably cynical view of life. He owes his origins to an author named Dashiell Hammett, who, before he took up writing, worked as a private detective. His employers were Pinkerton's – a firm which, on the last reckoning, was the biggest private detective agency in the world.

Pinkerton's were founded in 1850 by a Scottish emigrant to the United States. Throughout the company's history, they have solved cases which have baffled the proper authorities. That scourge of the Wild West, Jesse James, was tracked down by a Pinkerton man. During the American Civil War they formed what was, to all intents and purposes, the beginning of the United States Defence and Intelligence Agency. On one occasion, they recovered a Gainsborough painting which had been stolen from a London gallery. And they put more train robbers, bank robbers and jewel thieves, behind bars than can be counted.

Nowadays, most of their criminal work has been taken over by the Federal Bureau of Investigation, but Pinkerton's continue to be very active indeed. Among their clients is the Jewellers' Security Alliance, and it was on behalf of this organization that they came into contact with Willie the Actor. Willie was known to his parents as William Francis Sutton, but he never wore one name for very long at a time. As his nickname suggests, he played many parts – and assumed many different aliases.

M. Rosenthal and Sons were a firm of jewellers whose premises were on Broadway, New York. At 8.45 on an October morning in 1930, a young man wearing the uniform of a telegraph messenger rang the doorbell. The porter, who had been making himself some coffee at the back of the shop, shuffled up to see who it was.

'Telegram!' said the young man.

The porter pulled back the bolts, and unlocked the door. It was then that he noticed that the messenger was not alone. Standing behind him was a handsome man wearing a tweed suit.

Instead of handing over the message and waiting to see whether there was any answer, the young man pushed past into the shop. He was followed by the man in tweeds, and the porter became unpleasantly aware that the latter had a gun in his hand. They beckoned him to the back of the shop, where they tied his wrists together with picture wire. Then they sent him back to the door.

'The staff ought to be arriving soon,' the bogus telegraph messenger said. 'Let anyone come in who has a right to.' And, to make sure that he carried out these instructions, the man in tweeds remained beside him, playfully scratching his back with the gun.

During the next few minutes, fifteen assistants arrived. Each of them was greeted with unimpeachable courtesy and ushered to the back of the premises. Nothing unpleasant would happen to them, they were told, provided they kept quiet.

When the last member of the staff had arrived, the porter was brought to the telephone. The young man in uniform dialled the employer's number. 'Find out what the combination of the safe is,' he said. And the gun wagged a warning barrel. The old man did as he was told.

When the two intruders left the store, they had 129,000 dollars' worth of jewellery with them. They climbed into a car which was waiting outside and, before anybody could go after them, they had vanished amid the traffic. One of the assistants took the car's number, but it was of no avail. As one might have guessed, it had been stolen.

The case was reported to the Jewellers' Security Alliance, and this body immediately called in Pinkerton's. Thereafter, the private detective agency and the police worked together on the inquiry.

Detectives searched the store for fingerprints, but both men had been wearing gloves. They then produced photographs of a number of crooks who might have been responsible for the crime. Could the staff recognize any of them? The porter and several others immediately pointed to the rather mournful face of Willie the Actor.

The detectives were not surprised. Dressing up in a uniform was just Willie's style.

Nobody could pick out a face which resembled the other man. Willie, it seemed, had found a new friend – and one who had never been convicted.

Knowing that Willie the Actor was responsible for the crime was one thing. Finding him was another. It was some time before an officer happened to see him driving a car. It was not possible to stop him, but the patrol man got the number.

After a tedious search through the files, the car was found to be the property of a lady who lived in the western part of Manhattan. Police detectives and Pinkerton agents kept watch on the house, which was inhabited by an attractive girl and her baby son. They followed the girl wherever she went and did their best to remain unseen. It was an easy assignment. The young woman obviously had no idea that she was under suspicion.

One afternoon she led the detectives to a cafeteria. Sitting at a table in the window was Willie the Actor. The girl joined him.

This was a delicate situation. Willie was a charming person who enjoyed a joke. His manner was always extremely polite but, if he was cornered, he was liable to become dangerous. The detectives had little doubt that his well-dressed exterior concealed a gun somewhere. A shooting match in a crowded cafeteria would be disastrous.

More detectives and agents were called on to the scene. The idea was to keep people away from Willie's table. It was cleverly done. Some blocked the aisles, appearing to be looking for unoccupied seats. Others filtered in seemingly engrossed in reading newspapers.

One played the part of a drunk. Gradually, without giving away any clues to their real identity, the network of the law closed in on Willie. Presently, there was a detective on either side of him. Each man held a revolver.

The girl looked terrified, but Willie smiled at her. There was not, he assured her, going to be any shooting. They quietly left the premises and fifteen minutes later were sitting in the detectives' room at the local police station.

Willie was a great one for playing different roles, and he could be an amusing conversationalist. At times like this, however, he was a good deal less than communicative. The detectives plied him with questions, but he said nothing. As always he was extremely courteous about it. He quite saw the detectives' difficulties, but he was sorry – he couldn't tell them anything.

The girl, on the other hand, had a great deal to say. It turned out that she was Willie's wife. Shortly after the Rosenthal robbery, he had settled the sum of 2,000 dollars in trust for their son. He was a kind man, she said. A good father. Very nearly the ideal husband – apart from his occupation. They had been married for over a year, and she had been under the impression that he was a salesman. It was, perhaps, understandable. Few wives are prepared to be sympathetic to their husbands when they come home tired after a hard day's stealing.

Could she, the detectives wondered, give them any clues about Willie's accomplice? She thought not, except ... well, there was that day's outing to Providence, Rhode Island. On their way from Manhattan Island, they had gone over a bridge. After a while, the road went under the railway and, presently, her husband had stopped the car outside a laundry. He had got out and gone into a building three doors away. Presently, he had returned with a good-looking young man, whom he called Mark. Mark had spent the day with them.

The next fortnight was typical of crime investigation. To find the right bridge, the right railway line, and then the right laundry. That was really something. But, in the end, they got there. The building had a downtrodden look about it. There was a bar on the ground floor, and the rest of it was a cheap boarding house. The landlady told them a man called Patterson answered to Mrs Sutton's description of 'Mark'. He lived on the third floor.

Mr Patterson had departed but, fortunately for the detectives, he had left all his belongings behind. There were all manner of uniforms, four pairs of hand-cuffs, 3,000 rounds of ammunition, countless revolvers and sub-machine-guns, a gas mask, pamphlets on gun silencers, a detailed floor plan of the Rosenthal shop on Broadway, a list of that firm's employees, and a collection of car number plates. It was sufficient to keep a small army of crooks in full time business for the rest of their lives.

All this was very interesting, and certainly showed that Mr Patterson had been involved in the jewel robbery. It was not until the detectives got down to the bottom of a large trunk, however, that they found any clues as to where he might be. The first was a bill for the hire of costumes to the 'Waverly School of Drama'. The second was a scrap of paper with an address in Buffalo on it, and a note saying: 'I will be in Buffalo to spend Christmas dinner with you . . .'

Christmas was still some weeks away, so this could

wait. In the meanwhile, there was the Waverly School of Drama to be investigated. Had Willie become so obsessed with his nickname, that he had decided to instruct others in the art of acting?

The so-called school turned out to have offices on Sixth Avenue. A notice announced that it was 'under the direction of J. W. Patterson'. That, indeed, was about all that could be said of it. The doors were locked; the rooms were empty; it had, the detectives established, gone out of business on the day after the costumes had been delivered. It was nothing more than a delivery point for the uniforms Willie used as part of his robbery technique.

A visit to the firm in Philadelphia, which had manufactured the four pairs of handcuffs, turned out to be equally disappointing. An executive told the investigators that, improbable though it might seem, this company had received 100,000 orders for this type of merchandise from citizens living in New York. To find out further details about Mr Patterson's delivery would take ages.

The only hope now was that the mysterious Mr Patterson would keep his Christmas date in Buffalo. The local police were alerted, and they picked him up on the day before Christmas Eve. True to the descriptions, he *was* a tall, handsome man, and he was wearing a tweed suit. His real name was Marcus Bassett. He came from a respectable Buffalo family, and had been educated at Syracuse University. After graduating, he had tried to make his way as a poet and short story writer. When this failed, he fell in with Willie the Actor and took to crime. What with his imagination and Willie's histrionic ability, they were a formidable combination.

The police picked him up on the day before Christmas Eve

Unlike Willie the Actor, who had learned how to keep his mouth shut when the occasion demanded it, Bassett made a full confession. He said that he and his accomplice had been responsible for eight hold-ups and had stolen 214,000 dollars worth of goods. But, when they sold it to receivers in the New York underworld, it only fetched 25,000 dollars.

In May of the following year, he and Willie were each sentenced to thirty years in Sing Sing. Bassett seemed to accept it with resignation. Willie, on the other hand, was heard to say 'there's no jail that can hold me' as he went through the prison gates.

He was right – up to a point. One year later, he escaped. He cut through the bars of his cell and climbed over the wall using a scaling ladder. He was caught again in 1933, after he had robbed a couple of safes. This time he spent thirteen years in jail before he got out again.

During this period, he had made four attempts to break out, and was nearly drowned during one of them – when he tried to wriggle out through the sewer.

For the next five years he remained at large. This time, he was re-captured as the result of a tip-off by an informer. Shortly afterwards, the man was murdered. Willie was never convicted of the crime, but the court made sure that he would be put away for good. According to one estimate, his accumulation of sentences was so large that he would not be due for release until the year 2087. Since Willie is now seventy-one, it seems unlikely that he will live to see the day. As his friend Marcus Bassett said with more sincerity than originality when he signed his confession: 'Crime doesn't pay'.

SIX

THE LONG CHASE

Adolf Eichmann was a tall, thin man with large ears and receding black hair. He was also a murderer. The exact number of his victims is not known. He once said that there were five million of them, but this is probably a conservative estimate. Six million is more likely.

He was not a killer in the sense that a gunman, a strangler, or a poisoner is. He never met most of his victims, but that did not lessen his guilt. He murdered them just as surely as if he had fired a machine gun at them.

In 1941, Field-Marshal Hermann Goering produced what he described as the 'Final Solution'. The Nazi party, of which Goering was one of the leaders, had always been against the Jews. Goering's idea was to exterminate them: to wipe them off the map of Europe.

And Eichmann was put in charge of the plan.

He worked from an office. Sometimes he visited the concentration camps. He dotted the 'i's and crossed the 't's. In his painstaking way, he administered the crime which Goering had dreamed up. The fact that his work was almost unbelievably evil did not seem to occur to him. He excused everything by pointing out that he was merely carrying out orders.

What orders! The master plan of a maniac! It did not seem to bother Eichmann.

Adolf Eichmann

In April, 1945, the war was almost over. Eichmann, like the other Nazi war criminals, was on the run. He visited his home in Austria for the last time. His wife afterwards recalled that he had slapped his eldest son. 'I thought this was the best way to part with him – by implanting some discipline in him,' Eichmann had told her.

From his home, he went to see the head of the secret police, who was hiding out in a village in the Austrian Alps. He found the man playing patience and drinking brandy. 'What are you going to do?' he asked Eichmann. Eichmann said that he was about to round up a party of soldiers and go up into the mountains. 'I'll stay here,' the Gestapo leader said.

One hundred and fifty men were mustered. They took food with them and went to some huts above the snow line. They remained there for about a fortnight. Then they heard that Germany had surrendered.

'It's every man for himself,' Eichmann told them.

He himself found a uniform which had once belonged to an airman, second class, in the Luftwaffe. Calling himself Adolf Karl, he walked and hitch-hiked back to Germany. He was picked up by some American soldiers and taken to a prisoner-of-war camp. If they had looked at him more closely, they would have been less casual about him. The number of his blood group was tattooed on his arm. Only members of the SS, the Nazi élite corps, had that.

The camp was only loosely guarded, for there were millions of prisoners of war in Germany at the time. It served Eichmann's purpose admirably. He did what he had intended to do: rested for a few days, and then escaped.

Three months later he was again caught by the Americans. This time, he was wearing the uniform of a lieutenant in the 22nd Cavalry Division. He called himself Otto Eckmann. When the authorities asked him why he had no documents, he said that he had destroyed them. They believed him.

Throughout this period an intensive search was going on for Adolf Eichmann. But there were a great many other war criminals wanted in what Lord Avon described as 'the biggest man hunt in history'. It never occurred to anyone that the quiet, rather withdrawn, Lieutenant Otto Eckmann might be one of them.

Presently, he escaped again. One of the prison camp inmates was a skilled forger. He faked up some documents for him, which gave his name as Otto Heninger. When he was clear of the camp, he changed into civilian clothes. Then he started to look for work.

He found a job surprisingly easily – as manager of a small chicken farm. It was horribly ironic. The police and soldiers of several nations were looking for him. And here he was, all the time, right under their noses. His farm was within a few miles of one of his most notorious concentration camps.

But this could not go on for ever. There were two organizations which helped ex-Nazis to escape from Europe. One was known as ODESSA (letters which stood for Organisation der SS Angehoerigen). The other was called Die Spinne (the Spider). They worked under the cover of perfectly respectable welfare organizations: indeed, many people who helped them had no idea of what they were really doing.

Eichmann went to one of them for help. He was put in a group of four men. They travelled by a route run by the Nazi underground through Austria and into Italy. Eventually, they arrived at Genoa, where they found sanctuary in a monastery. The good-natured Franciscan monk who gave Eichmann a passport with the name Ricardo Klement on it did not know whom he was helping. To him, Eichmann was just an anonymous person who needed help. The Nazi villain received his new identity on July 14th, 1950. Four weeks later, he landed in Buenos Aires. His papers described him as a German who had been born in Bolzano, Italy. They listed his trade as that of a mechanic.

Up in the north-west of the country, not far from the Andes, there is a town named Tucumàn. A construction firm had its headquarters there. It had sheltered a number of ex-Nazis on its payroll, and Eichmann (or Klement as he was now called) went there for a job. They signed him on.

He worked there for some time. Presently he began to feel so safe that in 1952 his wife and three sons joined him. The scent had grown cold: the hunt seemed to have been called off.

During the next few years, he managed a rabbit farm, worked for a business which exported jute extracts, and finally, in 1956, joined the Mercedes Benz organization in Buenos Aires. He lived in a small house on the edge of the city. He became careless about revealing his identity. He even told some of his associates that he was really SS Lt-Col Adolf Eichmann, retired. To some extent, he was right to feel secure. The United Nations War Crimes Organization had admitted that it had been unable to find him, and the Argentine authorities did not seem to mind who he was.

Two men were determined to bring Eichmann to justice. One of them was Tuvia Friedmann who lived in Vienna. The other was Simon Wiesenthal, whose home was at

Linz. Both men were Jews and both had survived the horrors of concentration camps. When they were released, they were too ill to walk. But, as they gradually recovered their strength, they dedicated themselves to hunting down the man who had tried to exterminate their race.

There was no lack of helpers. Jewish refugees from all over the world were anxious to do what they could. Eventually, their efforts were coordinated by the Israeli Intelligence Service, which had its central office in Tel Aviv. But there were precious few leads. The one contact that Eichmann seemed to have in Europe was his wife. Like Wiesenthal, she lived in Linz. Was there a possibility that, one day, he might come out of hiding and visit her?

They made their moves delicately. First of all, they planted a girl as housemaid in the home of some friends of the Eichmanns. There was a rumour that these people acted as a link between the Jew killer and his wife. Nothing happened. There were not even any letters from the wanted man – which would have given a clue about where he was living. The only hope was to get inside the Eichmann household.

Vera Eichmann had no reason to suspect the pleasant girl who struck up an acquaintanceship with her. Her three sons – Klaus, Hans and Dieter – seemed to like her. She played with them and told them stories, and listened to them. Gradually, Vera Eichmann began to trust her. No doubt she was lonely. At all events, the girl became a regular visitor to the house. She took the children for walks each day, and sometimes took them rowing on the lake. What Mrs Eichmann did not know was that every evening the girl spoke to Wiesenthal. And, always, her story was the same. Adolf Eichmann had made no move to get in touch with his wife.

Presently, Vera Eichmann moved to a smaller house in another part of Austria, and this part of the operation was called off. In the meanwhile, Friedmann was dealing with a large correspondence. Some of the letters were anonymous. They said that unless the search was abandoned, Friedmann would be killed. There were also communications from men who offered to sell him details of Eichmann's whereabouts. Like the threats, these ended up in the wastepaper basket. Friedmann had decided that they were all the work of confidence tricksters.

And, just like flying saucers, reports came in of sightings from various parts of the world. Over a relatively short period, Eichmann was variously said to be in Kuwait, Egypt and Damascus. There was not a word of truth in any of them.

When rogues fall out, they make a thorough job of it. One of the most improbable offers came in 1946 when, had they but known it, Eichmann was still hiding behind one of his assumed names in a prisoner-of-war camp. The man responsible for it was another SS thug named Wislinceny, who had been one of Eichmann's assistants. Unlike his master, he had been rounded up and was awaiting trial. In return for his freedom, Wislinceny offered to track him down.

'One has contacts, you know . . . one understands his habits . . . I would find it easier than most investigators.' No doubt: but this sudden and unlikely ally of the Jewish people had committed enough crimes of his own. They decided that he should remain in jail.

More reports came in. Eichmann was in West Germany, Syria, Turkey, Spain. In every case, agents who had been sent to the countries concerned reported that there were no traces of the man. The identification always turned out to be a mistake – or a hoax.

Friedmann presently moved home to Israel and, as Eichmann had guessed, the investigation reached an apparent dead end.

In 1958, the West German Government set up a department in Ludwigsburg which was known as the Central Office for the Prosecution of National Socialist Crimes. The object of it was to gather evidence against all Nazis who had not yet been charged with offences against humanity. Among the men in charge of it were eight judges. Acting through the Ministry of Justice, the director told the Israeli authorities that they would be glad to exchange information. The Israelis accepted the offer with thanks.

Nothing happened for over a year, and then, out of the blue, came a tip from West Germany. According to a reliable foreign source, Eichmann had been seen in Buenos Aires. He was now called Ricardo Klement, and he was working at the Mercedes plant.

The Israeli authorities were now in a dilemma. Eichmann had made a wise decision when he escaped to the Argentine. Most countries have extradition treaties with each other. This means that if, say, a person flees to France after committing a crime in Britain, he can be brought back to stand trial. But there was no treaty between Israel and Argentine concerning the surrender of war criminals. If Eichmann was to be found and captured, and if he was to be brought to Israel to stand trial, the whole operation would have to be conducted unofficially – and in strictest secrecy.

An agent was immediately sent to Buenos Aires. He was a Hungarian whose family, including his parents, had been killed by the Nazis. Miraculously, he had escaped. It almost seemed as if he had been preserved to carry out this task.

He had little difficulty in tracking down the Klement home. Casual questions to the Mercedes workers gave him all the information he needed. Nor was there any difficulty in identifying Mrs Eichmann (who was now called Mrs Klement). Her photograph had been taken several times when she was living in Linz. The problem was to be sure that she really was living with Eichmann. For all they knew, this man Klement might be some harmless character who had nothing to do with the case. After all, Vera Eichmann had been without a husband for nearly fifteen years. Wasn't it only natural that she should assume him dead, and marry somebody else?

There was, of course, that report they had received from Germany. But, then, there had also been those false accounts from so many other sources. Whoever was responsible for it might have assumed that because Vera Eichmann was there, so too was Adolf Eichmann. Or, as so often happened, the informant might have made a false identification.

Matters would have been made very much easier if the agent had been given a photograph of the wanted man. None was available. Unlike the author of the 'Final Solution', Hermann Goering, who preened into the lens of any camera which happened to be pointing in his direction, it seemed as if Eichmann was shy of photographers. Shy – or, perhaps, prudent.

This investigation had been difficult from the start. It did not become any easier as it progressed. Eichmann was a wily bird, a villain who seemed to slip through any net intended to capture him. Whatever must be done had to be handled with extreme care.

But, in one respect, the Israeli agent was lucky. There was a room to let in one of the houses which overlooked the Klement property. He rented it. Before very long, he was rewarded with a sighting of Mrs Klement (still Mrs Eichmann in real life?) and the children. It seemed that she now had four sons. Was the latest child Eichmann's, or did he belong to an unknown Argentinian whose name really was Klement?

The agent had equipped himself with what seemed to be a good cover story. He let it be known in the neighbourhood that he was the representative of a British firm which manufactured sewing machines.

It was in this capacity that he called on one of the Klements' neighbours. Her husband was out at work, and she invited him in for a cup of coffee.

'Are you selling sewing machines?' she asked.

The Israeli agent said that he was not. 'My company has decided to open a branch in Argentina,' he told her. 'We want to build a factory, and we would like to build it here. It would be good – wouldn't it? Just think of all the jobs that we would create. This would become one of the most prosperous suburbs of Buenos Aires.'

No doubt. The lady agreed that the prospect was a very pleasant one, but she didn't see how she could help.

'Just this,' the agent said. 'We would need land for our factory. Would you be willing to sell us your house?'

'I suppose so,' the lady said. 'Providing the price was good enough.'

'Excellent. I wonder how your neighbours would react. Klement, I think their name is?'

'Klement – yes. I don't know. I could ring Mrs

Klement up and ask her. I don't think that she has gone out.'

This was not exactly what the agent had in mind. He had hoped to lead the woman round to a conversation about the neighbours: what they were like, what kind of man was Mr Klement, when did he usually come home from work? – that sort of thing. However, since the good lady had suggested making a phone call, he did not see how he could stop her. Perhaps it did not matter in any case. Wasn't it logical that a British sewing-machine company might be contemplating putting up a factory?

'She says that she'll have to talk to her husband about it,' said the over-willing helper, putting down the telephone. 'I can't guess what he will say. The Klements don't mix with the rest of us very much. They aren't very forthcoming.'

'Do you know much about them?'

'Well – I think they are German. Or used to be. I'm not sure what he does. Works at a car plant? A garage? I'm not certain.'

It was not a great deal to go on, but the agent had to be content with it. He went back to his lodgings.

During the next few days, he caught glimpses of Klement as he went to work and came home in the evening. But they did not tell him much. The light was bad and the man might have been anybody. It was not until the Sunday that he had any luck. It was a sunny day, and Klement was working in his front garden. The agent was able to take the man's photograph using a camera with a telephoto lens.

Having done this, he paid the balance of his rent, and caught a flight back to Israel. He never realized how close the well-meaning neighbour's phone call had come to defeating the whole operation.

Klement (or Eichmann as he really was) heard about it from his wife when he got home that evening. 'What would they want with a place in this remote suburb?' he asked. And then he reminded her that they were not even connected to the municipal water supply of Buenos Aires. It all seemed extremely improbable.

Perhaps he had been safe for too long. It was now eight years since he had crossed the Atlantic to South America. During this time he had been unmolested. His defences had grown soft. He even talked too much. One of his colleagues at work had been heard to remark that it was ironical – one of the most powerful men in Nazi Germany reduced to making parts for motor cars. It had almost become a joke.

His suspicions about the sewing-machine project melted away.

'I expect they were simply making a rough survey,' he said.

Then he forgot all about it.

The agent's film was developed in Tel Aviv. He had taken some excellent photographs – but of whom? They showed the head of a man who had a thin face, large ears, a pronounced nose, an unremarkable mouth, and thinning black hair. Eichmann? There were people who had seen him; but it had all been a long time ago, and under horrible circumstances. And Eichmann must have looked younger then. He had more hair. His face was not so thin. They thought it might be him. But, well – it was difficult. They were not sure.

An agent operating in Western Germany had the job

of going through files of old magazines. In one of them, there was a shot of Eichmann at some Nazi gathering. It was not a particularly good picture, but it was all there was. He brought it back to Israel.

To the layman's eyes, it was almost impossible to see whether these two men were the same. They sought the help of the police, who put an expert on the job. He studied both photographs, checking this point and that, looking for common features, but even he was uncertain. He was prepared to say that there were no contradictions – which meant that they could both be of the same man. But he was not prepared to make a positive identification.

More agents were drafted to the Argentine. Before deciding what to do next, they had to be absolutely certain that they had found the right man. Among them was a gentleman named Molnar, who had met Eichmann several times in Budapest during 1944.

Early on in his stay, Molnar picked up a clue at a cocktail party. Somebody referred, quite casually, to the fact that Eichmann was working at Mercedes-Benz. The tall man with the large ears who lived in the suburbs and was called Klement was identified leaving the factory. He was trailed on the bus to his home. But the final word came from an Argentine government official. In return for a fairly large sum of money, he confirmed that 'Yes – Klement is Eichmann.'

When the news reached Israel, it caused considerable argument. Some factions believed that a summary execution of the Jew killer should be carried out on the spot. The idea was enormously dangerous, for it, itself, would involve an act of murder. What is more, it made a mockery of all civilized ideas of justice. People might know that Eichmann was guilty of his crimes. But it had not been proven before a court of law. Would not this be adopting the very barbarian behaviour that most of the world condemned? This, as somebody pointed out, was the progressive state of Israel – not a branch office of the Mafia.

Most people agreed that Eichmann, whatever kind of monster he was, should have a fair trial. The difficulty was getting him to Israel. The Argentine Government, obviously, would do nothing to help. Quite apart from the question of extradition the existing authorities knew all about his presence there, and seemed to be perfectly happy about it. Hadn't it been necessary to bribe a senior official to support the rather flimsy evidence of identification?

Somehow, the man had to be smuggled out of the country.

So far the investigation had not been unlike a conventional police case involving Interpol. Literally, thousands of people had been questioned. Informers had come forward. Some had been cranks, some had been hoaxers, and some had made mistakes. The same thing happens when the police are handling things. There had been a good many false trails and, when at last they were on to something, the evidence had to be checked and re-checked. It was not very different from the methods of Scotland Yard.

But, once the police have made their arrest, there is seldom any difficulty in getting the accused to the police station. They certainly do not have to kidnap the man, smuggle him through the passport barriers, and then fly him several thousands of miles to another country.

At first, the idea seemed to be impossible. It might be feasible to land and take-off unseen in a light aircraft.

To travel all the way to Israel, on the other hand, would require something very much bigger. They would have to use a recognized airport. If Eichmann kicked up a fuss on the way out, the whole mission would have to be aborted. Kick up a fuss? He'd do more than that. He'd raise hell. The authorities would come to his rescue: say, 'You mustn't take away our poor Mr Eichmann.' They would probably end up by arresting the Jewish agents.

By a stroke of good fortune, the traditions of Argentina itself provided the answer. During the month of May, this country celebrates the anniversary of its first Government. It is a very happy occasion, ranging from sober speeches at one end of the scale to revelry in the streets at the other. There are carnivals, and music, and dancing, and for several glorious hours the machinery of government is relaxed.

One of the concessions of the occasion is that, throughout the public holiday, all customs and immigration formalities are relaxed for aircraft coming into the country. It is as if Argentina has left the front door open. Everybody's welcome, the message seems to read.

Consequently, nobody took much notice of a Bristol Britannia airliner which landed at Buenos Aires on May 24th, 1960. It was said to be on a charter flight, but few people cared. This was the first day of the celebrations, and the airliner might have been on a mission to the moon. Nor, when it took off again at midnight on the following day, did the officials pay particular attention to it. They might have wondered why it was carrying an exceptionally large crew, or else an unusually small number of passengers. In fact, it seems very unlikely that they knew how many people were travelling.

But, before this a lot of things had been happening . . .

In April 1960, four crack Israeli commandos had landed in Buenos Aires. They spent the next two weeks studying Eichmann's movements. They found that he was a creature of habit. He always went to work on the same bus, and he always returned home at the same time in the evening. He got off at a bus station down the road, and walked the last few hundred yards to his house.

On May 11th, the weather had taken a turn for the worse. It had rained for most of the day. In the early evening, it stopped, but the sky remained overcast. Only a few people were out in the street.

Eichmann stopped work at the usual time. He joined the queue of Mercedes-Benz employees at the bus stop; climbed on to the vehicle; and about half an hour later reached the bus station. He buttoned up his mackintosh, and set off down the road. He did not seem to notice two black saloon cars which were parked by the pavement between the bus station and his house.

Suddenly two men accosted him. Eichmann reached into his pocket. Thinking that he was about to draw a gun, they sent him flying to the ground. He struggled for about five seconds, and then one of the commandos knocked him out. He was carried into the car which made off at full speed to a small farmhouse which had been rented for the operation.

In fact, Eichmann did not carry a gun. It was not his style. He was fumbling for a flashlight to see who the two men were.

He was held captive in the farmhouse for two weeks. During this period, he admitted who he was. He said that he was prepared to stand trial for his crimes in either Argentina or West Germany. The Israeli commandos laughed. They pointed out that he did not have very much say in the matter. But, they insisted, he should sign a paper, declaring that he was leaving Argentina of his own free will, and that he was prepared to be judged by the due process of Israeli law.

'I'm tired. My head's aching,' Eichmann said.

They told him he could rest. Several hours passed, and then Eichmann came back into the room. 'All right,' he said. 'I am prepared to proceed to Israel to stand trial.' The time was just past midnight.

Adolf Eichmann was tried on fifteen counts before a court of judges in Jerusalem. Throughout the proceedings, he sat in a bullet-proof glass booth. From time to time, his normally impassive face twitched slightly. Otherwise, he betrayed no emotions.

He pleaded for clemency, and fell back on the traditional Nazi defence that *'Befehl ist Befehl'* ('orders are orders'). The judges found him guilty. Eichmann had once said that he would die happy in the knowledge that he had dispatched five million enemies of the Reich. Now it was his turn to be dispatched. He was hanged in 1962.

SEVEN

RED FOR ROBBERY

Shortly before 7 PM on August 7th, 1963, a train pulled out of the Central Station, Glasgow. There were no passengers on board, for this was a travelling post office. It made the journey between Glasgow and London every night – peopled by hard-working men who sorted the mail as they rushed down the length of Britain. The second coach from the engine was known as the 'high value package coach'. It was here that consignments of banknotes were carried.

There were two unusual features about the train which left Glasgow that night. One was that the previous Monday had been a bank holiday. There had been a big spending spree in Scotland, and the high value package coach had an exceptionally large amount of money on board. The other was that the top-security coaches, which were normally used, were being overhauled. Consequently, the train was made up of older stock which could more easily be broken into (in fact, it would have been almost impossible to invade the normal rolling stock).

At 12.30 AM, the train pulled into Crewe on time. The drivers changed over, and fifty-eight-year-old Jack Mills settled down at the controls for the rest of the journey to Euston. He was accompanied in the cab by a fireman, David Whitby.

The train called at Tamworth and Rugby to pick up more mail; and, at 3.15 AM, they were racing through Buckinghamshire at 70 mph. As they approached the signal gantry at Sears Crossing, about thirty-nine miles from London, Driver Mills noticed that the red light was showing. He put on the brakes, and the train presently came to a stop.

At the foot of the gantry, a telephone is connected to the nearest signal box. Mr Mills asked his fireman to phone through and find out how long the delay was likely to be. He suspected that it was caused by electrification work which was being carried out.

Mr Whitby clambered down to the track. He walked over to the gantry and found the telephone. Nobody answered. Then he realized that the wires had been disconnected. As he went back to the train, he noticed a man standing behind the second coach. He thought that he was probably one of the post office sorters, and he asked: 'What's up, mate?'

The man walked towards him. He pointed down the embankment, and said: 'Come over here.' Mr Whitby then saw that he was wearing overalls and a balaclava helmet which acted as a mask. Suddenly, the man gave him a push. He fell backwards down the bank, and found another character waiting for him at the bottom. This man overpowered him, and muttered something about 'If you shout, I'll kill you.'

Mr Whitby surrendered. He was taken back to the train.

Meanwhile, in the driver's cab, a battle had been raging. Another bandit, who was also dressed in overalls and a balaclava helmet, had appeared on the steps carrying a long stick. Jack Mills attacked him and, for a short while, he seemed to be winning. He was a tough, determined, individual, who had the advantage of being on more solid ground than the bandit – who was perched somewhat precariously on the step.

But the battle did not last long. Another man had entered the cab through the far door. Now he hit Mr Mills from behind. The engine driver went down on his knees. He was then battered on the head by both men. Surprisingly, he never lost consciousness. But the train robbers had made their first mistake. They had intended to use as little violence as possible. Mr Mills had received injuries from which he never completely recovered. Somebody, and they never found out who, had exceeded his instructions.

Mills and the fireman were handcuffed and taken to a passage behind the cab. More men, all of them dressed in balaclavas with a couple of holes for their eyes, now climbed on to the engine. There seemed to be a good deal of discussion going on. After a minute or two, one of the bandits helped Mills to his feet. He was made to drive the engine and the first two coaches, which had been disconnected from the rest of the train, half a mile down the line to a bridge. When they reached it, he and Whitby were handcuffed together: made to climb down to the ground, and told to lie by the side of the rail. One bandit stood guard over them.

The job of disconnecting the coaches had been carried out so efficiently that neither the guard nor the post office sorters realized that anything was amiss. Delays on this section of the line were quite common at the time. They thought nothing of it, and carried on with their work.

Once this portion of the train had reached the bridge,

however, it was a very different story. About fifteen raiders smashed the windows of the high value package coach, and cut their way through the sides with axes. The men were all armed with coshes (there were no guns). Against this severe opposition, the postal workers did not stand a chance. They were made to lie down on the floor in a corner while the bandits formed a human chain, passing the mail bags down to the embankment, and then to a fleet of transport which was waiting beside the road. When all was done, the thieves had robbed the train of £2,631,784's worth of bank notes.

Mr Mills and Mr Whitby were put back in the cab, and told to do nothing for half an hour. A similar warning was given to the sorters in the coaches. In fact, once the mail bags had been loaded on to the trucks, nobody was left behind to see that the instructions were obeyed.

The guard, who had been left behind with the remaining nine coaches, eventually sounded the alarm. They seemed to have been at a standstill for an unusually long time, and he walked up the track to see what had happened. When he saw that the engine and the front two coaches were missing, he placed detonators on the rails to warn other trains. Then he walked on towards the bridge. As soon as he saw what had happened, he stopped a passing train and was taken to Cheddington Station. It was there that he reported the robbery.

The 'Great Train Robbery', as it came to be called, captured the nation's imagination. The American magazine *Life* offered Ian Fleming, author of the James Bond books, a large sum of money to write an article about it. Mr Fleming, who was just off on a holiday to Switzerland, declined.

It came to be called 'The Great Train Robbery'

Two firms in the City, who were in the insurance business, offered £200,000 for information which might help the authorities to find the missing money. The Midland Bank offered £50,000 and the Post Office, less generously, was prepared to pay £10,000. As might have been expected with such big incentives at stake, a flood of stories poured in. Scotland Yard had to set up a special sorting office to deal with them – only to find that most of them were useless.

Things reached such a pitch that more or less anyone who flourished a five-pound note was suspected of being a train robber.

A lorry driver was said to have been seen throwing parcels into the Thames from Vauxhall Bridge. Nothing was found in the river. The police were informed of two men who were seen digging a hole at Lyndhurst golf course in Hampshire. When questioned, they explained that they were preparing the foundations for a new club house. When a horse box was thought to have been abandoned at Reigate, Surrey, people rushed to the conclusion that it was full of pound notes. In fact, it had a flat tyre, and the owner had gone to a garage.

At a small shop on Anglesey, a man bought some post cards and a fourteen shilling bathing costume. When he was paying for them, the assistant noticed that he had a wad of five-pound notes. 'Are you one of the train robbers?' she quipped. The man was seen to tremble. He dropped his money on the floor; picked it all up apart from a £1 note which he overlooked; and departed in confusion with a woman who was waiting outside in a Dormobile. Later, he turned out to be a perfectly harmless holiday-maker.

Tip-offs even came from as far away as Mar de Plata in the Argentine where anyone who spoke English and gambled at the Casino came under suspicion. The underworld, naturally, rallied to the banner of law and order in the hope of earning some of the reward money. Praiseworthy though their intentions may have been, they did not help the police in the slightest. And, for a period, it seemed as if no public-spirited citizen was capable of enjoying a few drinks in a pub without feeling himself compelled to telephone the police about the train robbery.

Nevertheless, in spite of a mountain of useless information, a few items came in which were extremely valuable. The most important was from a herdsman named John Maris, who worked on a farm some miles from the scene of the crime. During the course of his duties, he had to go near a place called Leatherslade Farm. The farmhouse had been empty for about six months and then, suddenly, it was sold. Mr Maris' suspicions were aroused by the fact that a number of vehicles were parked in the yard and in the outbuildings. He noticed a green Land-Rover and a pale-blue Morris – and, in one of the sheds, there was a lorry. It was half hidden by a tarpaulin, but Mr Maris noticed that it had a yellow body.

Although the place was obviously occupied, he had never seen the inhabitants. Indeed, the windows were all covered with canvas sacking. Mr Maris found it hard to believe in a family that preferred to spend all its time in darkness, and never ventured out of doors. Consequently he informed the police at Aylesbury. No doubt because they had such an overwhelming mass of data to sift through, his message was overlooked. He telephoned them again on the following day, and he would have done so a third time – but he was frightened of making a fool of himself.

Unfortunately for the train robbers, the authorities took action when they received his second call. A team of twenty detectives, many of them specialists, came to Leatherslade Farm in ten cars, and started taking the place apart. They found the remains of meals (mostly baked beans), heaps of empty beer cans, piles of cigarette ends, and a half finished game of Monopoly. In the garden, there was a half-dug pit, in which somebody had been busy burying empty mail bags. The robbers themselves had departed, and it seemed that they had left on the previous night. The vicar of the village of Oakley suffered from insomnia. When his wife got up in the night to make him a cup of tea, they heard three lorries travelling very quickly along the road to Bicester. There was, perhaps, nothing surprising about this – except that the drivers were not using their headlamps.

Had the Aylesbury police taken action when Mr Maris made his first telephone call, they might have found Leatherslade farm inhabited. Now the place was empty except for the debris of a few days' occupation by what appeared to have been about fifteen people. However, this, in itself, told a story. The robbery itself had been a beautiful bit of work. Most people admitted that. The only mistake had been that of slugging the driver. If the villains were ever caught, it was bound to add years to their sentences.

After the crime, however, the organization seemed to have gone completely to pieces. During the occupation of the farmhouse, all the crooks should have worn gloves. That was so elementary that it hardly belonged in the same world as such a sophisticated and well planned crime as this. But the thieves had overlooked this precaution completely. There were prints everywhere – even on the Monopoly board and on a saucer of milk which had been put out for a stray cat.

This did not surprise the police. They knew that the most important part of a crime, from the villain's point of view, is *after* it has been committed. The criminal has been through a period of considerable nervous tension. He wants to become legal again: to escape from the scene of his misdeeds. It is best summed up in the words: 'Christ – let's get out of here!'

Unless he is very careful, he relaxes too soon. Was this, then, why Leatherslade Farm had been left in such a mess? Had the discipline, which had prevailed before and during the crime, broken down? Presumably the thieves had used the buildings as a base from which to mount their operation – and somewhere to share out the money afterwards. But then – what? Did the fact that they had not worn gloves suggest that somebody had been detailed to stay behind and clean up the premises? Possibly, he was supposed to burn them down, leaving no traces at all. And had he taken fright and departed, without carrying out his duties?

The police were not particularly concerned about this, for they now had proof of who the villains were.

Earlier on, they had suspected certain people. This was partly because of the very nature of the crime. The men had to be professionals: villains with a lot of experience, who went for the big stuff, and who were capable of assessing the gamble. Furthermore, a crime such as this required a fairly large capital outlay. The services of other criminals, each one an expert in a particular field, had to be retained. The fleet of vehicles could probably be stolen, but a place such as Leatherslade Farm had to be bought. Who had come into a good deal of money lately?

One case stood out. That was a daring robbery which

had been carried out at London Airport on November 27th of the previous year. The sum of £62,000 had been put on a trolley at the airport bank, and wheeled to the lift by security men. Three men, wearing bowler hats and carrying brief cases, were also waiting. They looked like perfectly normal businessmen, and the security officers paid no attention to them.

When the lift arrived, five men stepped out. They were all masked and, helped by the 'businessmen', they overpowered the guard. The £62,000 was rushed to a pair of stolen Jaguars which were waiting outside. The cars were driven with considerable skill flat out around the perimeter road to a gate, which was forced open. Thereafter, all traces of them were lost.

A number of men were suspected of the crime. One of them was Charles Wilson. The police turned up at his home in South London, only to find that Mr Wilson was taking his three little girls to school. When he returned, they were waiting for him at the door.

'Oh Christ!' he said. 'What's it all about?' Then, to his wife: 'Mum – get in touch with my mouthpiece. It's the Law.'

He asked them whether they had time for a cup of tea before going to Cannon Row police station.

The case against him never got very far. He had an alibi which, as it happened, was never needed. Nobody could identify him sufficiently and he was never brought to trial. Douglas Goody, a hairdresser, was also suspected of being involved with the airport robbery but he, too, was dismissed through lack of positive identification.

Eventually only one man was convicted of the crime. One of the last things he said to the police was: 'At least

I shan't get done for the big job.' Big job? Could this be the train robbery?

There was also the case of a solicitor's clerk named Bundy. Mr Bundy had a habit of talking a good deal, sometimes rather too loudly. On one occasion, he claimed that he knew the names of all the people behind the robbery. Shortly afterwards, he was found unconscious at Oxford Circus tube station in London. After ten days in a coma, he died. Or had he been murdered? Eventually, the detectives satisfied themselves that he had not been.

All the while, the people were asking whether there was a master mind behind the robbery. A man who, as you might say, never got his hands dirty; who planned the operation and then gave others the task of carrying it out. There was talk of a house in Brixton where, behind blacked-out windows, the robbers used to have weekly meetings. At these, it was said, a mysterious Mr 'X' briefed them about their assignment.

There were also reports of a house in Earl's Court, which was said to have been used for a similar purpose. When the police raided it, they found that it had been empty for three months. And there were accounts of how one of the bandits had picked up the basis for the plot in prison. One of his fellow inmates had heard about the idea – the author of which, or so some people said, was a wealthy business man.

Planning crimes, the rumour had it, was his hobby – rather as some people enjoy working out chess problems. It was, presumably, more profitable.

But the police were inclined to dismiss these ideas. They considered that it was essential for the planner to take part in the actual raid. After all, criminals are not noted for their obedience. Somebody has to keep them in order.

If all this was somewhat in the air, there was nothing vague about the conversation which took place between a barrister and one of the heads of Scotland Yard. It was at just about the time that the police received Mr Maris's communication about Leatherslade Farm. The two men met in a West End club. The barrister told the senior policeman that one of his clients wished to do a deal.

The individual in question was serving a sentence in prison. He had been convicted just before the train robbery, and he claimed to know the names of all the thieves. In return, he hoped that things might go better for him, and that he might eventually be put on parole. But, he insisted, his name should never be made public. Even the name of the jail was not to be divulged.

Were the authorities interested? The officer said that they were.

The visit to the prison was carried out rather like a piece of cloak-and-dagger work. The detectives did not use a police car for the journey, but rented one from a hire firm. Even the warders believed that they were prison visitors and had nothing to do with the police. They said that one of the inmates had asked whether he might consult them on 'a personal matter'.

At first the informant was vague. He seemed to be uncertain about the names of the villains, and referred to them by their nicknames. Although he may not have realized it, this made things easier for the police. Criminals change their identities fairly frequently, but their nicknames tend to remain constant. For this reason, the criminal records at Scotland Yard include an index of them – just as they include a list of the underworld's girl friends. This, too, turned out to be useful; for in one case, the convict could only remember the name of the man's fiancée.

When he had been talking for a while, he seemed to become more confident. He explained how they had recruited specialists to help with the technical side of the crime. There was, for example, an electrician on the gang's payroll. His job had been to make sure the train came to a halt. He did it by fitting a glove over the bulb which illuminated the 'go' signal. So that the 'stop' signal stayed on, he wired up a special circuit, using four dry-cell batteries.

The robbers had also received tuition in how to uncouple coaches, and a contact (he was not sure who) had been hired in Glasgow, to inform the gang which train would be carrying the banknotes.

One member had been promised £100, if he stayed behind at the farm and burnt it down after the others had gone. He, obviously, had been scared, and that was why the detectives had found so many fingerprints.

The evidence was now coming in thick and fast. Having discovered Leatherslade Farm, the police turned their attention to finding out how it had been acquired. The previous owner had been a gentleman named Bernard Rixon. He had bought the place as a smallholding, and had sold it during the month before the crime. His solicitors had handled the matter: his only contact with the purchaser had been to meet a man whom he described as well dressed, well spoken, and altogether charming. He had fair hair, and he did not seem to be a countryman.

After the deal had been completed, a farmer called round. His cattle had been in the habit of grazing on land belonging to Leatherslade Farm, and he wanted to know whether this arrangement could continue. It was a sunny day, and two men were in the garden. One was sitting in a deckchair; the other was lying on an inflatable mattress. Both were wearing shorts.

When he put his question to them, they replied that he would have to wait until the owner was there. They had simply been employed to redecorate the place.

The farmer was suspicious. He had been inside the farmhouse and had seen that it was in good condition. It did not seem to be in any need of redecoration. Later, he reported this visit to the police.

But the really important feature of the sale of Leatherslade Farm was the name of the purchaser's solicitors. It was the same firm that had represented the defendents in the London Airport robbery case. This, surely, was too much of a coincidence.

The man in charge of the train robbery investigation was Chief Superintendent Tommy Butler, who died of cancer in April, 1970. One of his former colleagues has said that: 'Nobody was really close to him: he was a difficult man to get to know. I think, basically, that he was shy. But, for everyone that hated Tommy Butler's guts, there was somebody who loved him. He would never ask an officer to do what he wouldn't do himself. Somebody once described him as a "soft character with a hard centre". I think this was true. He used to arrive at the office at about eight-ish and he quite often used to go on working until ten at night. He was a bachelor who never smoked, though he'd take a drink. I think, really, he lived for his work and for his old mother.'

This, then, was the man who had the unenviable task of tracking down one of the most intelligent bands of men who had ever carried out a robbery. Once he had received the list of names from the informer, he checked them against the tally of prints found at Leatherslade Farm. They corresponded in all but one case. One man's prints were missing. Was he the only one who had bothered to wear gloves?

It was now a question of rounding up the suspects. The first arrest was made as the result of a phone call from a lady in Bournemouth. Two men had called at her house with an A35 van and asked whether they could hire a lock-up garage. She thought they were holiday-makers, and told them that the rent would be fifteen shillings a week. When one of the men asked whether he could pay her for three months in advance, and then started to peel off five-pound notes, the lady became suspicious. She telephoned the local police, who came round immediately. The moment the men saw them, they started to run. One of them lost a shoe in the process. The chase did not last long. When the two men were safely in custody, the back of the van was examined. It was found to contain £141,000.

Shortly after this, a Surrey man was giving a lady a lift to work on his motorcycle. It was an old model and, on the way, it over-heated. He parked it in a lay-by opposite Redlands Woods, near Dorking. While they were waiting for it to cool off, they took a stroll in the woods. To their surprise, they came across two holdalls and a briefcase half hidden under a bush. They called the police, and one of the police dogs sniffed out a suit-case. They were all stuffed with five-pound notes.

Two days after that, a caravan belonging to one of the suspects was found abandoned. The sum of £30,000 had been ingeniously hidden behind the walls.

£242,207's worth of the stolen notes had now been recovered. More came to light in, of all places, a

London telephone booth. It almost seemed as if, with so much of it in their possession, money had ceased to have any meaning for the criminals. It had become just a large collection of pieces of paper.

A network was thrown out for the wanted men. In some instances, the police did not have to look very far. Charles Wilson, for example, was found behind the yellow front door of his home at Clapham.

Roy James (the Weasel), whose prints had been found on the saucer of milk put out for the cat, was a racing driver – and a very good one. Two days before the robbery, he had won an event at Aintree in his Formula Junior Brabham Ford. He was entered for a race at Goodwood on the following Saturday, and turned up to practice on the Thursday. With a speed of 95.57 mph, he put up the fastest lap, and would have had the commanding position on the starting grid.

Working on the assumption that he would not be able to resist the chance of winning a race, detectives turned up at the meeting. They piled into the paddock and around the pits but Roy James never turned up. They captured him four months later after a chase across the rooftops of St John's Wood.

One of the leading suspects was the hairdresser, Douglas Goody, who had been detained and questioned about the London Airport robbery, and then released for lack of evidence. He had left home and had been living in a room above a public house. On August 23rd, he broke cover, and went to visit a girlfriend in Leicester. He was picked up at the hotel where he proposed to stay. Instead of a pleasant night's sleep in one of the city's most expensive establishments, Mr Goody spent the time until 6.30 on the following morning being questioned at the local police station. The young lady he had been to see was also interrogated. Why, the police wanted to know, had she £25 in her possession, and how could she account for the £2,250 mink-covered studio-couch in her home? The explanation turned out to be completely innocent. She had won both the money and the couch in a local beauty competition that had been held on the previous Wednesday.

The prosecution of Douglas Goody turned out to be the most controversial aspect of the case. Whatever the others might have said, there was no denying the evidence of the fingerprints at Leatherslade Farm. Goody, on the other hand, had taken the precaution that all the others had ignored. He had worn gloves. There was absolutely nothing at the farm to link him with the crime.

Why, then, had he been hiding? He said that, as soon as news of the train robbery had been published, the press had regarded him as one of the suspects. Reporters had made a nuisance of themselves, and he had taken this room in order to escape them.

But, when the police were questioning him at Leicester, other officers were searching that room. They took away with them a pair of suede shoes. On them were minute particles of yellow and khaki paint. The Press made quips about 'Goody Two-shoes', which is the title of a children's play; but Douglas Goody found nothing to laugh at. Scientific tests proved, to the satisfaction of the jury which eventually tried him, and to the judges who turned down his subsequent appeal, that this paint had come off a lorry and a Land-Rover which had been found at Leatherslade Farm. Apparently they had been repainted to disguise their appearances. Some of it must have rubbed off on to the unfortunate Goody's shoes.

One by one, the robbers were rounded up. When, in

January of the following year, twenty of them were put on trial at Aylesbury, there was one notable absentee. His name was Bruce Reynolds. He was described as an 'antique and car dealer', and the last trace of him was a black Austin-Healey sports car which was discovered in a street near London Airport.

A man who resembled the description of Reynolds had bought the car on the day after the robbery. He had paid £835 for it in fivers – but, the salesman insisted, there was nothing unusual about that. Most of the customers who paid cash for their cars settled in five-pound notes.

He drove it to a garage some miles away, and asked if he could park it there. He had, he said, a plane to catch. That was the last they saw of him. The car was eventually moved out into the street, for it was cluttering up the garage's forecourt. Whoever owned it never came back to collect it.

The police checked the passenger lists at the airport, but these were of no help. Later, the West German police reported that a plastic surgeon in Hamburg had been visited by a man who looked like Reynolds. He had offered £9,000 in sterling for a quick operation that would change the shape of his mouth. The surgeon said that he would have to think about it. The man left a hotel telephone number. When the police went there, they found he had made a hurried departure.

Eventually they caught Bruce Reynolds: not in Mexico or in the West Indies, or any of the other far-flung places where he was said to have been seen, but in Torquay. When Chief Superintendent Butler arrested him, he said: 'I was wondering when you'd come.'

The train robbers received some of the harshest prison sentences that have ever been meted out in

Britain. The ringleaders, which included Charles Wilson, Douglas Goody, Roy James, and Bruce Reynolds (when he was finally brought to trial) were given thirty years each. Understandably, the sentences were severely criticized. On the one hand, they were thought to be unreasonably brutal. On the other hand, they were said to encourage violent crimes. If a man received such a long sentence for robbery, why should he stop at murder? He had nothing, surely, to lose?

But the law decided that there *were* worse things which could befall a criminal. When a thief was tried, some years later, for the killing of a police officer, he was sentenced to remain in prison for the rest of his life. And, the judge emphasized, *all* of it. For him, there would be no remission.

As Marcus Bassett had observed somewhat tritely thirty-two years earlier: 'Crime doesn't pay'.

True Adventures and Picture Histories